"I entered into Sara Easterly's [...]
which it is, to be sure. What I [...]
speak to me so personally. S[...]
memoir about adoption. Beyo[...]
our common quest for wholeness, meaning, connection, belonging, and truth. Sara explores these deeply universal themes with unflinching honesty, authenticity, and vulnerability, which means this book will speak straight to your heart and soul — whether you are an adoptee or not."

— **Michelle DeRusha,** Author of *True You: Letting Go of Your False Self to Uncover the Person God Created*

"A touching story of raw daughter-mother attachment with all its imperfections and heartaches, together with surprising twists and redemptive forgiveness. It rings true because it is truly delivered."

— **Gordon Neufeld, Ph.D.,** Founder, Neufeld Institute, and best-selling author of *Hold On to Your Kids*

"Fiercely personal, Sara's memoir exposes the cracks in her formerly sugarcoated adoption story. Sara perseveres in seeking the truth, revealing the painful wounds of adoption loss. We follow her journey to healing with both her mothers, which unexpectedly culminates in a newfound understanding of God's mothering."

— **Haley Radke,** Creator and host of *Adoptees On* podcast

"Sara has written a disarmingly honest memoir about pursuing truth — truth about herself, her faith, her family, and even truth about her pursuit of truth. She beautifully conveys that a genuine pursuit of truth becomes the soil in which healing love grows. A worthwhile read from beginning to end."

— **Richard Dahlstrom,** Senior Pastor of Bethany Community Church and author of *The Map is Not the Journey* and *The Colors of Hope* — named a Best Book by *Christianity Today*

"A beautiful piece of work. Sara speaks the truth in this book and the truth sets people free!"

— **Sundee Frazier,** Award-winning author of *Check All That Apply* and the *Cleo Edison Oliver* series

"Sara Easterly has created a fearlessly beautiful story of a daughter's search for a kind of perfect love she actually — in the end and much to her own surprise — finds."

— **Anne Heffron,** Author of *You Don't Look Adopted* and founder of *Write or Die*

For Sarah— With love for your motherhood journey!

Searching for Mom

A MEMOIR

SARA EASTERLY

WITH LINDA EASTERLY

Sara Easterly

HEART
VOICES

Published in the United States by Heart Voices
2400 NW 80th St #257, Seattle, WA 98117

Names: Easterly, Sara, author.
Title: Searching for mom: a memoir / Sara Easterly
Description: Seattle, WA: Heart Voices, [2019]
Identifiers: ISBN 9780578601953
Subjects: Easterly, Sara—Family. | Christian biography. | Adoption. | BIOGRAPHY & AUTOBIOGRAPHY / Memoirs. | Mother-infant relationship. | Mothers and children. | Death. | Adult children—Family relationships. | Adult children of aging parents—Family relationships. | Adopted children—Family relationships. | Christian life. | Parenting. | Child development.

Scripture quotations marked (MSG) are taken from THE MESSAGE, copyright © 1993, 2002, 2018 by Eugene H. Peterson. Used by permission of NavPress. All rights reserved. Represented by Tyndale House Publishers, Inc.

Scripture quotations marked (ESV) are from the ESV® Bible (The Holy Bible, English Standard Version®), copyright © 2001 by Crossway, a publishing ministry of Good News Publishers. Used by permission. All rights reserved.

Scripture quotations marked (NIV) are taken from the Holy Bible, New International Version®, NIV®. Copyright © 1973, 1978, 1984, 2011 by Biblica, Inc.™ Used by permission of Zondervan. All rights reserved worldwide. www.zondervan.com The "NIV" and "New International Version" are trademarks registered in the United States Patent and Trademark Office by Biblica, Inc.™

Scripture quotations marked (CEV) are from the Contemporary English Version Copyright © 1991, 1992, 1995 by American Bible Society, Used by Permission.

ISBN: 978-0-578-60195-3 (print)
ISBN: 978-0-578-60470-1 (eBook)

Printed in the United States of America
10 9 8 7 6 5 4 3 2 1

For Violet and Olive

Generation after generation stands in awe of your work;
each one tells stories of your mighty acts.

—Psalm 145:4 (MSG)

Table of Contents

PART 2: HONOR YOUR MOTHER

PART 3: GOD, THE MOTHER

TABLE OF CONTENTS

Introduction

You are the one who put me together inside my mother's body,
and I praise you because of the wonderful way you created me.
—Psalms 139:13-14 (CEV)

A few months after my mom died, my youngest daughter said to me, "You'll never know how you got here until you get to heaven." We were driving in the car after her morning at playschool, rounding the corner and almost home. I glanced in the rearview mirror to get a look at my four-year-old's contemplative face and those darling, inquisitive eyes.

"What do you mean?" I asked. "Got where?"

"You'll never know how you got inside Grammy's tummy," Olive said.

Uh oh. The birds and the bees talk … already? I reminded myself of prevailing parenting advice around this topic. *Whatever you do, don't answer more than she's asking. Wait to find out what this is really about.*

"But I was never inside Grammy's tummy." I'd only recently found my birth mother, so talking comfortably about my adoption was still out of my grasp—let alone my four-year-old daughter's. But I figured sticking to the facts was in order. "Remember? Grammy adopted me. I was in Diane's tummy."

"Yeah, but … you'll never know how you got here," she insisted.

We pulled into the garage. I turned off the ignition. My daughter wasn't asking about sexual reproduction—nor the intricacies of adoption.

11

In her childlike innocence and wonder, she was tapping into that innate spiritual awareness I believe we're all born with. And while my daughter wasn't technically accurate, her reflections were right. I don't really know how I got here.

I had figured out the key story elements. There was an adoption—a "grey-market adoption" with shady circumstances. A young birth mother had been pressured into giving up her child—not so unusual for the era, where patriarchy and lack of regulation wielded its weapons of shame over unwed young mothers. An eager adoptive mother was desperate to have a child. Tension was created by a joyous, but complicated, mother-daughter relationship with years of unspoken feelings and layers of secrets. The ticking clock, or deadline for closure, loomed, while the mother was dying at the too early age of sixty-six, due to complications with her autoimmune disease, polymyositis, and two sets of lungs that ultimately failed her.

But how did I ultimately land with the family that raised me? How did I finally come to welcome children into the world myself, after years of proclaiming that I'd never subject another generation to this frightening, dark place? These questions may seem like a mid-life cliché, but the circumstances behind them have shaped my life in substantial ways and, when studied through the rearview mirror, they reveal that it has been an exquisite and divine symphony. Like many stories of spiritual deliverance, though, that was only clear on the other side of forty years—a number Rachel Held Evans has described as carrying special significance. "Rather than an exact enumeration of time, forty symbolizes a prolonged period of hardship, waiting, and wandering—a liminal space between the start of something and its fruition that often brings God's people into the wilderness, into the wild unknown."[1]

Thankfully, as my mom was dying I was gifted a conversation to hold on to—a heart-to-heart conversation with God that made sense of my life and the way it came together.

Shortly before she died, I sat at Mom's bedside with a longtime friend of hers, Nancy, who reminisced about the time when her daughter and I, aged nine and ten, had rolled our eyes and said, "You guys are way too immature to be mothers." I hadn't remembered this episode in our lives until Nancy reminded me. As a daughter, I made note of a lot of Mom's imperfections. There were plenty of "oh, mother, you're so embarrassing!" remarks. And there were silent disappointments, like being hurt when she got the facts wrong in stories about me, so I wouldn't fully listen to what she had to say, as a result. I didn't always give her a lot of grace to fall short.

My scrutiny intensified once I became a mother, determined to make up for my mom's shortcomings and protect my children from any suffering I experienced. Every day I worked so hard at being "the perfect mother." Yet, as I became all too aware of the many ways I fell short of my ideal, I wondered which of my imperfections and missteps would land my children on a therapist's couch—or, if they were like me—send them looking for other mothers somewhere else.

What I didn't realize until my mother's death launched a spiritual epiphany is that it takes a lifetime of being a mother to mature and reach perfection. We all seek unconditional love and the invitation to exist in another's presence exactly as we are. I didn't always feel that from my mom. Sometimes I said or did things that got me in trouble. And I was so sensitive I could read her disappointment in the slightest upward tilt of her eyebrow or the most subtle shake of her head.

But the process of my mom dying showed me that nobody can give us that perfect invitation.

That is, nobody except for God.

In the meantime, though, Mothers are the next-best thing.

This book is an attempt to share my story, to answer the question of how I got here. I'll confess, though, that I'm what they call in fiction writing an unreliable narrator. How can I not be, as a memoirist and a human? I've tried to write my truth as accurately as possible, but capturing memories is elusive. My biases, immaturity, and imagination can't help sweeping along on the voyage, no matter how much I strive for truth. "Memory is not always an accurate recorder of truth. It changes over time," explains Nancy Newton Verrier.[2] For this reason I've interspersed the book with my mom's poetry and letters in an attempt to show more than my limited perspective.

While I'm on the topic of truth-telling, please note that out of sensitivity to some of the people I'm writing about, I've camouflaged their names and identifying details. These matters aside, however, this is my truth, my answer, my story.

Still, it's not the complete story. My daughter is right. I'll have to wait for that. "We may wish for answers," Rachel Held Evans wrote, "but God rarely gives us answers. Instead, God gathers us up into soft, familiar arms and says, 'Let me tell you a story.'"[3]

Here is mine.

PART I

Mother Longing

The Lord is near to the brokenhearted
and saves the crushed in spirit.

—Psalms 34:18 (ESV)

CHAPTER ONE

Taking Flight

We who are strong have an obligation to bear with the failings of
the weak, and not to please ourselves.
—Romans 15:1 (ESV)

Monday morning. I'd flown home to Seattle, back from Denver long
enough to toss dirty clothes out of their suitcases and start a load of
laundry. While my two daughters reacquainted with their dolls and
Magna-Tiles, I recalled my mom's response when I'd told her that
I planned to return to Denver for another visit the following week.

"Oh. I'm not sure I'll still be here then, Sara." Mom started to say
goodbye.

I cut her off.

"No. I'll see you again." I smiled, trying to pretend this was any
other farewell. Trying to convince her—convince myself—that this
wasn't really The End. There was no way Mom was dying. I'd been
fabricating this kind of confidence about her life for the last five
years.

But goodbye was in Mom's eyes. Goodbye was in her embrace,
weak as it was, even though I'd grown accustomed to "air hugs" —
lest I spread germs to her highly susceptible lungs and body.

Suddenly, I felt sure of nothing. I faked my way back to life-as-
usual on the plane ride home, barely able to process anything my
children were saying. I was Mama-on-Autopilot, dragging carseats
off the plane, lugging weary bodies into the car and then inside the
house, washing airplane crud off tiny hands. Not that any of this was

unusual. Numbed-out mom dutifully attending to the needs of small people while furtively fixating on a swirling emotional storm was one of my specialties.

I needed to talk to someone so I called a close friend. Heather had been through this herself, when her mother died a few summers earlier.

"You're back in Seattle?" she asked skeptically, confirming my unease.

"Yes, but I'll go back to Denver again next week," I said. "I told my mom I'm going to go back again next Monday."

After an awkward pause, Heather said, "I hesitate to tell you this, but the end can go pretty fast."

"Faster than a week?"

"I'm sure it's different for everyone," she said. "I just know it went really fast for my mom. I wasn't prepared for that."

Unsettled, I called my sister for reassurance.

"I don't know how to explain it, but there's been a change since you left," Amy said.

Even though we'd been home for less than an hour, I moved full throttle, rebooking a flight back to Denver that would leave in two hours. After dropping Violet and Olive off at a friend's house, I sped my way through childcare and scheduling plans while en route to the airport—calling my in-laws, the preschool teacher, babysitters, and my closest friends and neighbors.

For a moment, I paused from the grim matter at hand to applaud myself. As a new parent I'd learned about the importance of a support village—something often lacking in this isolating age without live-in grandparents or "aunties" next door, and thanks to a fleeing-from-church culture. Mindful of this, and in lieu of in-city grandparents and church-based community, I'd deliberately worked to surround my family with our own "village." *Look at those efforts pay off!* I told myself.

All the week's plans came together as I rounded my way into the parking garage at SeaTac airport. My husband Jeff, who'd been on a business trip, would land in Seattle within thirty minutes of my flight's departure out of Seattle. That left just the right amount of overlap for me to hand him the car keys, tell him he'd find the car in row 5J of the parking garage, text him the week's schedule for the kids, and kiss his stunned face on the cheek.

As an event planner by trade, I'd always been a master of logistics. But I usually spent months working on each event. This rushed effort surpassed anything I'd attempted before. *Did I have help on my side?* I wondered, and then caught a flit of an answer: *Maybe this is the kindness God doles out when your mom is dying.* In any case, the fact that everything lined up so effortlessly and would be so gentle on my daughters, made me think that I was flying in the right direction. I just hoped I'd get there in time.

More importantly, I hoped to be up for the challenge. Mom had been preparing for her death for the last four months, but that didn't mean I had.

Sure, I'd read *Final Gifts: Understanding the Special Awareness, Needs, and Communications of the Dying* by Maggie Callanan and Patricia Kelley. I'd even bought copies for my dad, sister, aunt, and grandma. I'd read about a dying mother who kept appealing to her family with travel metaphors, but whose family didn't grasp that her last request wasn't literal, which created a lot of unnecessary anguish for everyone during her final days.[1] As a writer and reader, looking for meaning was right in my wheelhouse. I figured I'd be equipped to decipher any metaphors Mom might employ.

I'd also found out that dying people often converse with someone significant from their past who has already died, and how upsetting it can be for them if they aren't believed. According to Callanan and Kelley, family members are the most qualified to figure out any of the hidden messages that could come from one of these conversations.[2]

When I was in my twenties, my deceased grandfather visited me during a dream while I slept on the pull-out sofa at my grandma's place. It was a comforting dream, but the intensity of it began to pull me from sleep. My adored Papa was right there, I knew, and I fervently wanted to see him again. As my eyes slowly opened, I watched Papa's translucent shape, lying right next to mine, evaporate. The mystical moment, too, dissipated. For the next two days I pondered talking to Mom about it. I wanted her to help me understand this encounter I'd had with her father, but she was a self-described "fundamentalist Christian," and I figured she'd judge my spiritual experience as "New Age nonsense." When I finally worked up my courage and recounted the story, though, Mom urged me to call Grandma.

"She's been waiting for a sign from Papa," she said, "She'll want to know he's at peace."

Mom had helped me decipher Papa's hidden message, and I, in turn, planned to help her. *Maybe there's more mystery around death and dying than we realize.* I planned to be open to it, anyway. As Callanan and Kelley had said, "We can best respond to people who experience the presence of someone not alive by expecting it to happen."[3]

Expectant or not, this was mostly practical book learning — savory knowledge that fed my brain and my propensity as an adoptee to believe in far-fetched stories. My emaciated heart, meanwhile, beat with a hankering for more.

Because my heart knew that I'd been afraid to face the reality of Mom's declining health. I'd been too scared to speak important things that needed saying. I passed over vulnerable opportunities with jokes, denial, indifference, feigned confidence, forced control. I'd locked my feelings in a thick protective casing so I wouldn't have to deal with whatever I was supposed to feel when I thought about the rest of my life without my mom — while wrestling with memories of our last two tumultuous years.

Deep down, did I ever even accept her as my mother? I would miss her for sure. Perhaps more for my daughters, only four and five, who wouldn't get a chance to truly know her. But would it profoundly affect *me* when she was gone?

I felt so detached as I stared at the grey clouds outside the airplane window. But I'd vowed to give Mom *my* final gift: the peaceful death she deserved, the death a *Good Adoptee*[4] owed her, the death I felt I needed to give her to prove my appreciation and loyalty.

I reached under the seat for my laptop and began compiling family photos for her memorial slideshow. I planned to leverage my event-planning skills to pull together the funeral she never would have dared to dream up.

Turbulence began to agitate the plane — the tell-tale sign that the Rocky Mountains were behind us as we approached Denver. I gripped the arm rests of my seat as the plane jerked in the sky.

Pushing away my feelings to give Mom what she needed was my training ground for becoming a parent. Ignoring my needs helped me get the job done: Making dinner when I'd rather be lounging on the couch devouring a good book ... setting aside my own upsets or fears in order to soothe equally intense ones for my girls ... hiding my true feelings in the face of hopes and disappointments. This all served me as a mother, didn't it?

When I dared to look at the truth, I knew it served me as a daughter, too. It's how I'd learned to stay safe, keep Mom close. Dutifully choosing her needs over mine ensured that she'd never leave me. Surely that's where everything went so wrong, where I'd messed it all up, with my first mother.

Only Mom was about to leave me, too.

Images of being severed from her approached as fast as the plane slammed onto the tarmac. I thought about the pictures I'd just looked at—Mom's glowing face, delighting in me, proud of me. Would I ever exude that much love for my daughters, the way Mom overflowed with it for us? Could I be as present as she always seemed to be?

Remember her manipulation and lies, though, I reminded myself. *Her jealousy. Her mean streak. The last two years of mother-daughter turmoil because I broke the silence, stopped pretending* ... Those all told a different story.

A story I didn't want to end this way.

A story I didn't want to end at all.

I didn't want Mom to die, and I definitely didn't want our "us" to conclude before I could find the words my heart longed to say. I wanted to grow, become the person I yearned to be. A daughter—and a mother—who didn't act out of obligation, a girl whose heart wasn't unflappable, a human who dared to *feel.*

If only it were that easy.

CHAPTER TWO

Butterfly Deliverance

I was raised to be a church attender. I think it was expected that automatically made me a Christian. But, like someone once said, "Being in a church doesn't make you a Christian any more than being in a garage makes you a car."
—Mom, from her public testimony on becoming a Christian

I was out in the front yard playing on a hot summer day in Colorado when I discovered the huge yellow and black veined butterfly, a rare and special find.

As a seven-year-old, following a butterfly all over the yard that day seemed a completely natural thing to do. I imitated its flitting by skipping and twirling in the grass, following it from bush to flower and talking to it. To *her*. She stayed in my yard long enough that I'd appointed myself her friend.

After our jovial tour of all the shrubs Dad had planted the summer before, my butterfly headed past our mailbox, then toward the street. That's when I heard the sound of a car headed down the hill.

"Oh! Come back," I yelled. "Out of the street!"

But I didn't speak butterfly. My butterfly didn't understand human. I watched helplessly from the sidewalk as the car approached. The two seemed destined to collide. I squeezed my fists together in hopes that I could will the butterfly to flutter back to me ... or speed her up to reach the other side.

My fists held no hidden powers. I saw the potential for tragedy but had no control to stop it. As an extremely shy child, I didn't have the confidence to hold up my palm or get the driver's attention. I felt scared, tiny, irrelevant.

I watched the car's windshield crash into my beautiful insect friend as her wings got tossed in the air. The driver didn't notice, didn't even slow down. *What kind of person doesn't notice beauty right there in her face?* I wondered.

As soon as the car passed, I ran into the street.

In the wake of the car and its noxious exhaust, I found my butterfly friend. Not dead. But suffering. Her wings fluttered. Her antennae wagged in the breeze. I studied her eyes and swore she stared back into mine.

I knelt beside my butterfly friend. It was my first experience of a time warp. I may have been with her five or fifty minutes. Time became inconsequential. I talked to my friend, offering comfort and support. Each time one of her wings slowly flapped, my soul took flight for hers. "You can do it. Yes, try to fly!"

Eventually, I could no longer deny reality. My butterfly wasn't going to make it. Sticky gunk oozing out of her body glued her other wing to the pavement.

My role as friend deepened into that of comforter. "I'm so sorry this happened. I'm going to miss you so much." I promised not to leave her side until she died.

I kept my promise, gently petting her wing until it wasn't fluttering anymore, until I knew for sure my friend was dead. I felt her loss so deeply, the ache was so familiar, I was pretty sure I might die, too.

The Sunday after my butterfly died, Mom carted me straight over to the closest religious institution she could find to help me get over what she called "hysterical pet drama." She figured the best way to console her inconsolable daughter was through a Dutch Reformed church called Ridgeview Hills and the promise of heaven—only I had no context for heaven—or for church. Up until then, we'd only been to church on Easter and Christmas, or on weekends when Mom's parents happened to be visiting. For Mom, church seemed a good excuse to deck me out in Mom-sewn holiday dresses that coordinated with her pastel polyesters — less about church and more about a new, insecure adoptive mother's proclamation: "We're cut from the same cloth!" Surely our matchy-matchy outfits proved to the outside world that the two of us were a pair, that this mother-daughter team had bonded.

To me, church mostly meant playing with stubby half-pencils to scribble on offering envelopes — which felt so business-like, important — with their printed donation requests and X-marks-the-spot boxes. Church meant fun times scooting around the floor, analyzing the different shapes and colors of people's ankles and calves — once loudly reporting, smack in the serenity of a pastor's prayer, my delighted discovery of a woman's varicose veins. "Look, Grandma! This old lady has those purple lines on her legs, just like you!"

Ridgeview Hills had a children's program, graduating me from ankle-watching in the pews to Sunday School in the basement. Complete with peppy children's songs and a staged puppet show called Caraway Street, Sunday School was like watching my long-cherished Sesame Street performed live. Pretty awesome. On car rides home, I'd belt out catchy Jesus jingles and teach them to Mom. I learned the order of the books in the Bible — by staring in envious awe at the same girl who'd stand up every Sunday morning to rattle them off and score a candy prize. I learned about God, heaven, Jesus, and the Bible's most notorious duos: Adam and Eve, David and Goliath, Samson and Delilah, Noah and Ark.

On a mother-daughter church retreat, I repeated the words the leader told to us in order to invite Jesus into my heart. For good measure, and because the first time didn't seem to make much of a difference, I did it two more times at summer church camps, guided by counselors.

Did I walk away with healing, with new understanding of death and how to process grief? Did I come to a clear understanding of an after-life? Did I find out whether my butterfly would be waiting for me in heaven?

No.

My heart didn't seem to change, either. As I thought about it over the years, I wondered if those camp counselors weren't just a little bit crazy. One of them also taught us how to cast out demons. I didn't know what demons were, but it was pretty frightening to hear about. Yes, definitely on the freaky side.

Church, religion, Jesus. None of it seemed meant for me.

🦋

By the time I reached early adolescence, Mom was a full-fledged "born-again Christian." She dove in big—first with a Mothers of Preschoolers (MOPS) group, and then by starting a neighborhood Bible study.

"It's because of Sara that I found God," Mom would boast to her friends and religious cohorts. Sooner or later, she'd launch into a retelling of my butterfly story.

Her version usually sent me into a trance. Only the punch lines floated high enough to my ears.

"Well, one day Sara found a butterfly in the garage so she adopted him and named him Gregory ..."

I hadn't adopted the butterfly.

I hadn't named her Gregory.

"Unfortunately, despite all our efforts, the butterfly flew away at the first opportunity ..."

My butterfly did not fly away. She died.

"So Sara became hysterical ..."

Hysterical? The word is grief. Profound grief.

"I'd about had enough of the pet drama so I told her there was a butterfly heaven. She had no idea what I was talking about ... heaven? So I decided I'd send her to a Bible school at a nearby church ... the denomination was Dutch Reformed, which I'd never heard of. But, heck, they probably knew about butterfly heaven."

Then came the big wrap-up: How Mom's need to help me understand my butterfly's death was what transformed *her* into a Christian. How without me, Mom never would have found her loving Savior.

But where was the love in the story of a butterfly who suffered and died? Where was the love in a mother's flippant retelling – a mother who didn't bother with facts? Who stole something precious from her child by hijacking the story, transforming it into her own story of religious deliverance? Who couldn't even see her daughter in the story?

And why did my butterfly's death pain me so primally?

Was it because I, too – even as a carefree seven-year-old who'd never known anyone who'd died, who didn't even consciously understand she'd been adopted – had already known too much about suffering and death? Was I especially prone to sensing and empathizing anguish, having lived through it myself? Nancy Newton Verrier, an adoptive mother and psychotherapist focused on separation and loss in adoption, has referred to it as a common experience for adoptees in infancy, called "the death of the baby soul ... the overall feeling is a betrayal of the universe, of God, of the cosmos, of the infinite being. This was not supposed to happen. It is outside the realm of the natural order of life."[1]

Perhaps, also, I had unresolved anger: remnants in my wounded infant soul over other precious things that had been stolen from me.

Church began to change. No longer was it about having fun

and singing songs. Now it was an agenda Mom wore on her sleeve. She'd look at me with eyebrows raised whenever she caught me lip-syncing instead of belting out those high-pitched soprano notes she could easily hit. She'd invite my friends to join us, embarrassingly blatant in her desire to convert them.

We switched to a different church — a traditional Lutheran one — and throughout eighth and ninth grades I was forced to attend confirmation classes taught by the pastor every Wednesday night, in preparation for my first communion. I had to memorize, recite, and respond to things with big words I didn't understand. Catechism. Doctrine. Sacraments.

Every Wednesday, Mom and I would battle.

"I'm not going!" I'd scream. "I hate it there!"

"You don't have a choice," Mom insisted, and I would take my hate out on her.

She seemed oblivious to the adolescent's increased appetite for autonomy and for my drive to become my own person. She didn't realize I had a natural resistance to being told what to do, influenced, or directed from the outside. She didn't understand that when an adolescent doesn't know her own mind, she will want to push the objectives of others away.[2] And when it came to religion, I didn't know my own mind.

I thought Mom's church agenda was all about converting me, making me good, making me more like her, having grown up in the Lutheran church herself. It wasn't until thirty years later that I learned our sudden switch to the Lutheran church was wrapped up in my adoption. Mom wanted to honor my birth parents, who she had thought were Lutheran — the reason they picked her as an adoptive parent, she'd figured, since she'd been raised Lutheran.

I'd have liked to have known that. It might have made a difference in my interest in church. But Mom didn't talk about my adoption. She believed that my sole place of belonging was with her—and the church.

What she did not know was that whether I was in church or with my family, I felt like an outsider.

I was too shy, and too afraid of appearing dumb, to ask questions. My fellow confirmation students were strangers—confident, gregarious kids who had grown up in the church together, their friendships already formed and solid. I didn't belong. My insecurities and the social dynamics ate up ghastly proportions of my emotional and intellectual real estate.

Besides, I couldn't relate to the God I learned about—a God who seemed mad at me, a God I would never measure up to, a God who didn't want me any more than my birth mother had.

CHAPTER THREE

Unwanted

They want to blot me from memory, forget me like a corpse in a
grave, discard me like a broken dish in the trash.
—Psalm 31:12 (MSG)

I was nine when I stormed into my parents' room to rage at Mom.
Squeezed tight in my raised fist, my Mickey Mouse watch rattled as I
used it to pummel the air. Mickey's wiry black arms, capped with fat
gloved fingers, spun around the dial as I aimed the watch accusingly
at my mother's face.

"Look at me!" I yelled. "I can't even throw away this stupid
broken watch!"

"Sara, what are you talking about?" Mom asked, following me
into her closet as I ran to hide.

I slumped on the wall behind her clothes while I struggled to
speak—my face as red as Mickey's trousers. Being mad came easy.
Talking about the pain, though, was not.

Mom knelt on the floor next to me. "Honey, what is this about?
What's going on?"

"If I can't throw away this broken watch," I forced out through
my tears, along with the darkest thought I'd ever had, "how could
she just throw me away like that?"

She was my birth mother.

It was the first time that I dared to speak aloud the thought that
had haunted me ever since I'd begun to grasp that I'd been adopted:

I wasn't wanted.

I only remembered speaking with Mom about my adoption once, a few months earlier. She'd explained what adoption meant, only I didn't know what questions to ask. Like what did a "grey-market" adoption mean? Or why did my parents drive all the way to Billings in the middle of the night to get me? Why did Mom and Dad need to adopt a child in the first place? After all, three-and-a-half-years later they got pregnant naturally and Mom gave birth to Amy. I could have asked all this later, but I didn't dare. If living with nebulous thoughts of being unwanted and abandoned didn't kill me, the answers to my questions would surely do me in.

But I'd been organizing my room that day, picking through an array of kid-clutter to determine the keepers from the trash. The weight of it all began to drag me down. *My real mother tossed me away.*

"She was only fifteen years old," Mom told me. "That's so young, Sara. She was just too young to keep you." More was said. Like how she showed her love for me by finding a family for me.

Mom responded with what she thought were all the "right" things.

A few months later Mom had to reassure me again, after my neighbor Arlan teased me for being adopted.

"We *chose* you. You are special because you were chosen." And, "You've been with us for your whole life—you were only two days old when we adopted you."

Mom spoke from both a naïve heart and the reigning parenting advice for how to talk to your adopted child. But her responses weren't answering my real questions. Her words didn't satiate. They came across like adoption propaganda—and as I learned later in life, they indeed were. In fact, *The Chosen Baby* by Valentina Wasson was one of many similar books adoptive parents pulled from for their talking points, inspiring many an adoptive parent to borrow from comparable fairy tale-like stories. "The word *chosen* was meant to act magically on the child's psyche, dispelling all curiosity about the missing parts of the story," described psychotherapist Betty Jean Lifton.[1] But "unlike those familiar fairy tales of our Western culture, which are woven through time with truths of the human condition, the chosen-baby story is filled with errors of fact, improbable details, implied horror, as well as gaping omissions."[2]

Mom's chosen-baby stories haunted me. Bitter incantations rode the breezes of my unconscious.

Love means leaving.

Special means nothing.

Those first two days must have been terrible.

Nonetheless, I spent all of my childhood parroting the propaganda, like an unthinking, unfeeling drone. To some degree, when it came to my adoption, that's exactly what I became.

Once, a friend at school inquired with wide eyes about my being adopted, already running with fantasies of orphanages, foster parents, and perhaps even a mysterious twin separated at birth. I disappointed her need for mystery and intrigue. "Oh, it wasn't like that for me," I replied. "I've been with my family for my whole life."

The next time Arlan teased me for being adopted, the propaganda became my weapon. "Your mom didn't have a choice about you. Mine did!" I teased back, delighted by the shocked look that crossed his scrunched up, freckled face.

But "chosen" was nowhere near what I felt inside. Inside, I felt abandoned, discarded, unimportant.

After that day in the closet, I remained silent about my pain. But I spent a lot of time wondering about those first two days with my birth mother before my "whole life" began, and about the nine months I spent in her womb. *Did it really mean nothing to her? What were those two days with her like? Did she ever think about me? Would she ever look for me? Would she be able to spot me in a crowd?*

After the Mickey Mouse watch day, I kept quiet. Putting on the propaganda was so much easier than falling apart, than exposing my wounds, than listening to stories designed to argue with facts I'd already settled on:

At my very core, I was unlovable, broken. Unwanted.

CHAPTER FOUR

Storm Runner

Moses lifted his staff to the skies and God sent peals of thunder
and hail shot through with lightning strikes. God rained hail down
on the land of Egypt. The hail came, hail and lightning—a fierce
hailstorm. There had been nothing like it in Egypt in its entire
history.
—Exodus 9:23-24 (MSG)

Colorado had been a terrifying place for me to grow up. Summers
brought afternoon thundershowers nearly every day. Before the
storm warning could finish rolling across the bottom of the TV
screen, the cloudless cyan sky would be overcome by bulging,
bloated clouds the color of stone and soot. White, zigzagging bolts of
lightning spidered from the heavens, simultaneously reaching their
crooked fingers across the sky and down to the suburban prairie. At
the same time, heat lightning flashed in the sky like a giant's strobe
light. Thunder groaned and cracked—often only a hair's space from
a lightning strike, alerting us just how close each electrifying hit had
been. Sometimes large hail balls would hurl down from the sky, as
well, pummeling cars and decks and windows ... or people and dogs
who hadn't yet sought cover.

Many a tornado warning would sound at the golf course near
our house, alerting golfers (and, I surmised—me, too!) to seek shelter.
During one storm, I spotted six funnel clouds touching down on the
horizon, mere miles from our home. Another summer, while leaving
the Renaissance Festival, I looked up into a sage-colored sky and saw
clouds beginning to swirl right over the parking lot—and my head.

But natural disasters weren't the only terrors I faced as a child.

Our attic caught on fire once. Ash dropped from the ceiling into our pink bathtub below. The firefighters in their fat padded suits and masks scared me just as much as the fire did. I hid inside the hallway closet, peering through the crack in the closet door, watching them rush down the hall and violently attack the ceiling with their axes. It was close to ten frightening minutes before anyone figured out I'd disappeared. Then it was my worried mother's wrath that scared me, so I continued to hole up in the closet until a fireman—the wrong person—rescued me from my unconscious hide-and-seek game.

Summer fireworks shows unnerved me. I never could appreciate their artistry and beauty, being too worried about sparks landing on our heads. After my attempts to convince my parents to bring us back home didn't work, I'd hide under a blanket while the rest of my family enjoyed what to me really did look like "bombs bursting through air."

Everywhere I looked, it seemed I had no control over the world around me. I had no idea that as an adoptee I was predisposed to remain in survival mode, that "when trauma happens at such an early age, fear is part of the residue."[1]

Mom didn't understand it, either.

Even though Denver's afternoon storms (and my ensuing support needs) were somewhat predictable, Mom often wasn't at home with me when the storm alerts went off—she was usually out running errands with Amy. My choices were to retreat to the dark, formidable basement—otherwise known as home to Freddy Krueger—or brave the outdoor elements long enough to race to our neighbor's house down the street.

Our neighbor Marmee always welcomed me in, and sometimes she'd even agree we should wait out the tornado warning from her basement (also intimidating, but less so because of Marmee). When Mom returned home and then I did, too, she would laugh at me for running to Marmee again. She joked about it for years — never apologizing for not being there for me, offering a parent's reassurances, or even empathizing with my fear.

My fears not only grew stronger, but also became opportunities to pelt myself with shame. Obviously, I didn't enjoy being alarmed all the time. But I couldn't help it.

Even when Mom was at home, I felt alone. Thunderstorms would usually find me sequestered under our kitchen desk, covering the metal zipper on my pants with a pillow to thwart lightning from striking me. I'd watch, in a state of terror, as Mom's legs passed by in a flurry of activity. Only a few feet from where I huddled in need, she'd continue with her business — doing the dishes, wiping down counters, talking on the phone ... worrying me more as I fretted whether lightning could come through the phone line and zap my mom to death.

Sometimes Mom would respond to my concerns for her well-being with nonchalant statements like, "Oh, well. When it's my time it's my time." Now that I'm an adult, I can appreciate this perspective of acceptance. Aspire to it, even. But as a child very much dependent on her mother, Mom's casual attitude faced me into overwhelming emotions as I pondered the very likely possibility of her death.

Mostly, though, Mom thought my hiding, and the pillow cover-up, was hilarious. She'd rat me out to others in the family so they could poke fun at me, too. She'd chuckle with her friends about it. My fears became a joke, another "Sara Story" to tell. These stories, and laughing about them, continued well into my adulthood. They became family folklore.

Hiding under that desk during the storm, what I needed was a hug, to be wrapped up in my mother's love and light, to be told everything was going to be okay. I needed Mom to lovingly offer me her confidence, rather than laugh at my lack of it. My mother, though, because of intergenerational wounds passed down to her, was incapable of giving this to me.

For decades I awoke to recurring nightmares. Nightmares where tornadoes would be whipping wildly around, right outside our living room windows. But my parents wouldn't join me in retreating to the safety of the basement—and most notably, never provide me with tender assurances.

Later in life I'd realize these nightmares were echoes of my preverbal feelings as an infant and the emotions that overwhelmed me throughout my childhood. Grief, fear, confusion, anger—an ominous, rapidly rotating column of air that twisted and swirled around me, threatening to take me away, plop me in a faraway place as if I were Dorothy in *The Wizard of Oz*. But unlike Dorothy, who stood out in Munchkinland, nobody in my family noticed because I looked like them, talked like them, and dressed to precisely match them.

They kept going about their business. So did I. Acting like everything was fine. Pretending I'd never been adopted. Ignoring the tempest inside of me and all around me. The significant loss of my birth mother never acknowledged. The shadow of sadness cast over my childhood never seen. My feelings of being tiny and powerless, at the mercy of wherever the winds might take me—allegorically, the *Easterly* winds of my adoptive surname—never taken as genuine.

My anxiety spiraled into a vortex with even greater power. It wasn't safe to ask for help, to reveal my fears, to let down my guard.

I worked to create order out of my emotional chaos with handwritten spreadsheets cataloguing each of my "stuffed-up" animals and color-coding my closet. I tried to keep everyone around me close through excelling—winning spelling bees, endearing myself to my teachers. I worked to live up to my "special baby" story—performing on the piano, balance beam, and later, on the sidelines of the football field as a cheerleader.

I did whatever was necessary to keep running. Running from the storm.

CHAPTER FIVE

Ideations

He was despised and rejected by men, a man of sorrows and
acquainted with grief.
—Isaiah 53:3 (ESV)

It was an accidental suicide attempt. Even though I'd entered a long
period of death ideation, I never meant to take my own life. But once
the story started rolling, I couldn't locate the brakes.

Five months earlier, I'd broken up with my first boyfriend, Alan,
when I found out he'd cheated on me shortly after prom.

Alan was devastated over our breakup. His family life was bleak
and mental illness ran in his family. I'd been devastated, too—the loss
hurt so much I wanted to pitch myself into the laundry chute and die.
But when I held firm about our relationship being over, Alan was
first to try to kill himself by swallowing a bottle of pills.

When he called me from the hospital, my adolescent heart leapt
back to him. I felt terrible for breaking his heart. It shocked me that he
loved me enough for it to break in the first place. He'd been the one
to reject my love first, after all. But I'd always been a sucker for suffering, and not only for my butterfly friend. I could even empathize
with cans of baked beans at the grocery store, silently apologizing to
those poor cans not chosen when Mom needed me to grab only one.
It was never even a question whether I would accept Alan's desperate apology and support his return to life.

Alan spent the summer in an adolescent psychiatric center. I
spent much of my summer with my friend Maggie. After our shift

retailing at the mall ended, we'd hop into my VW Bug blasting Madonna songs on repeat. At a preappointed time well after dark, we'd drive to the parking lot of the psych ward. I'd flash my headlights at Alan's window, anticipating the twelve-second thrill of his silhouette waving back at me, abuzz with what I didn't realize was an all-too-familiar, primal longing for someone I could never possibly reach.

Maggie's love interest cleaned office buildings at night, so our next stop would be another parking lot. We'd wait there for a long time, trying to spot his shape pushing a vacuum cleaner while Maggie and I belted out our woes of unrequited love.

Unrequited love shading the summer or not, it was a carefree and happy time—some of my fondest memories of high school.

Alan returned home by summer's end with a psych degree, eager to share his enlightened analysis of me. Just as fall readied itself for winter, my season darkened, as Alan poked at my character:

"You're so shallow. You care too much about what everyone else thinks. You've bought into the system. Walking around school in your little cheer skirt. Showing off with your short flag friends. It's all so fake. You're not really happy inside. You're totally co-dependent. You need help."

Alan pricked on enough truth as he replayed all of the diagnoses from his own group therapy sessions that I began to doubt myself. *He was right. I wasn't truly happy. Had I ever been? Had I been faking it? And for how long? Maybe I hadn't really been as happy as I thought I was over the summer.*

When Alan shared about weekly sessions with his psychiatrist, I wanted that myself. *I need someone to talk to, too.* Thinking about my birth mother was near-constant, an intrusive, humming wonder that darted in and out of my consciousness—relentlessly all day, every day. When I first met Alan's mother—dancing in her tiny Boulder apartment, young and fun and without any apparent responsibilities or cares in the world—I'd wondered if she was *her*.

But I didn't have the nerve to ask Mom for a therapist. It'd been years since I'd authentically talked with her about my adoption. Speaking up would have felt like a betrayal. Instead of turning to Mom, I turned to partying. Then I'd "do weird things" as Alan had once reported to my mother. Those "weird things" are long forgotten now. What resides in my memory, though, is getting weepy and sad and generally feeling lonely, worthless, and hopeless.

Alan terrified my mother, who attributed my immense sadness solely to him, not grasping how much I *needed* that sadness. Without Alan, there was no other place, no other container. I'd been silently grieving the loss of my birth mother all my life. Now, as an adolescent, I felt additional loss pile on: the loss of my youth, my innocence, the loss that comes from simply growing up and separating from my parents.

Not that Alan was a pure vessel for my sadness. In addition to suicide, he introduced me to marijuana and LSD, and to the music of Ministry and Skinny Puppy (although much too satanic in appearances for my comfort). He drove recklessly on his motorcycle—a "crotch rocket," he called it—while I rode on back, squeezing my arms tight around his bodybuilder's waist. When my appeals to "Slow down!" only made Alan drive faster, I'd close my eyes and pray we wouldn't get killed—though sometimes those prayers were as scant and simple as "Oh, God!"

Mom invited him to join us at church, hoping to save his soul— for the sake of mine, more than his. Alan met us at church dressed all in black, donning his gothic black boots. He didn't sing along with the choir. He passed me notes and held my hand in the pew. Mom didn't invite him again.

When Alan and I broke up, Mom's relief wasn't well masked. She was there for me — offering comfort, empathy, and adult perspective — but I didn't accept or appreciate it, preferring to wallow alone in my room, listening to the most depressing songs by The Cure I could find.

Alan and I reunited. And broke up. And reunited. So went my senior year.

During one of our dramatic fights on the phone, I threatened to kill myself. The words came out of the ether. I'd been silently wishing to die for some time, but now I was outright saying so. Alan didn't seem surprised. Finally, I was admitting that I was just like he was. As a suicide veteran, I think he enjoyed knowing just what to do.

It felt like a part to play: the role of Suicidal Girlfriend. I hung up on Alan. Ran to get a bottle of Tylenol. Gagged down four or five before fear took over my impulsivity.

Alan called back, as I knew he'd do. But it surprised me and frankly wrecked my day when the paramedics arrived and whisked me to the hospital. My parents had to leave work to meet me there, and I missed my short flag cheer practice that afternoon. The whole squad found out. I had to drink charcoal juice as my stomach was pumped, nobody believing that I'd taken only a handful of pills.

I didn't know that I had become a statistic. Adoptees are four times more likely to attempt suicide than non-adoptees.[1] But I decided not to toy with attempting suicide again, even if for a shallow reason: it was too embarrassing. My life had always been about trying to fit in. Suicidal girlfriend was too distinctive a role for me. When I stepped out of my own perspective, I also felt guilty for the worry I caused my parents — especially Mom, who spent many, many years fretting whether I'd try it again.

But even as I vowed not to deliberately hurt myself, I flirted with a secret, unconscious hunger to come *close* to dying—usually only manifested when I drank. In college I'd discreetly bolt from parties at two a.m., then walk alone all over campus, imagining getting attacked. During a trip to New Orleans for an away game at LSU, I took off from my cheerleading squad, drunk and crying and lost—on the outskirts of the city, as well as on every possible level. On the freeway once, I opened the passenger door and "joked" to my hysterical friend Carrie that I would jump if she didn't get us home faster.

Weird Things, Alan would have called them, though we had broken up permanently by then.

Whatever my reckless actions were called, one thing was clear: I wanted to escape this painful world and my overwhelming sense of helplessness, this place where I felt so alone, where nobody rescued me—at least, not the one I kept hoping would.

A Letter from Mom

By Linda Easterly, to Sara

Sara,

I'm sorry about your rough day. I'm just glad it's over and you're OK.

I've been real worried about you because you've become so sad and so secretive. I want to reach out, but you're not ready so I will honor and respect your privacy.

For whatever is making you so sad—please remember that it can be fixed! Unfortunately, all these rough experiences in high school are somehow necessary for adult life. I truly don't believe there is a tougher time to go thru than high school! Friends don't sometimes stay loyal. Boys sometimes "DUMP"—school is just plain tough, etc.

I just want to reassure you that things will be OK, and I'll stand by you NO MATTER WHAT.

I'm praying for you and trusting that this particular set of problems will soon be behind you.

Mom

CHAPTER SIX

Secret Keeper

We're not keeping secrets; we're telling them. We're not hiding
things; we're bringing everything out into the open.
—Luke 8:17 (MSG)

I have always been a terrible liar. One of the obvious traits good liars
possess is an ability to keep secrets. But keeping secrets has never
been my forté. It's always felt wrong to hide things, especially from
those closest to me. As a very young child, I couldn't be trusted with
presents.

At the age of four-and-a-half, I helped Mom get a present for
Dad's birthday. "I can't tell you what it is, Dad," I beamed within
minutes of returning from the store, "but I'll give you a hint! K-A-
M-R-A."

The next year, Mom smartened up. In my presence, she would
only refer to Dad's gift as a "clicker." Of course, I promptly provided
him with this important clue—again and again and again, waiting for
him to guess it right. If he surmised his birthday present was a garage
door opener, for my poor mother's sake he didn't let on until after the
cake, once he'd ripped into the package.

It wasn't long, though, before I, too, learned to smarten up when
it came to secrets.

After kindergarten one day, Mom took my friend Nicole and me
to Safeway. While we waited for Mom to pay for the groceries just a
few checkout lanes away, Nicole pointed to a shelf of brightly colored
packs of bubble gum. Safeway had smartly positioned them right at

our eye level. They called out to us. "Psst! Over here! Bubblicious ... so deeeeelicious!"

Nicole grabbed a pack of Hubba Bubba. The strong scent of manufactured grape seeped through the purple package and Nicole's tiny fingers.

"Here," she said. "You should put this in your pocket."

"Okay," I said, not thinking much about it.

We watched Mom wheel her grocery cart past us and followed her through the automatic double doors. As soon as we reached the parking lot, I pulled the treasure from my pocket. Nicole smiled and we unwrapped two fat cubes of gum, popping the pure purple delight into our mouths.

I felt the ridges of the gum with my tongue, then took a bite, squishing it between my baby teeth. The flavor of grape filled my mouth just as we reached the car.

"Look, Mom! Gum!"

"Where'd that come from?" she asked.

I simply answered, "Inside the store. I took it."

In my eyes, that grape Hubba Bubba gave me sensory pleasure I never could have imagined existed. How grown up I felt, too, securing it all on my own! I couldn't wait to share the experience with the person closest to me — Mom, of course.

In Mom's eyes, though, I'd been caught — purple-handed. She was a God-fearing woman and, as any responsible parent in her shoes would, she'd better teach her daughter a lesson about stealing, right then and there! She marched me back into the store and sought out the manager. Insisting that I apologize to him for stealing left a huge mark on me, a child so shy I could barely look up to say hello to aunts and uncles, let alone strangers.

The worst part, though, was feeling how much sharing a secret could hurt. Over the years I became more and more private, especially when it came to things that really mattered, when the stakes were highest — the insecurities I felt about myself, my daydreams of the family I someday hoped to have, the fact that I wondered a lot about my birth mom.

By the time I was in high school, I'd had a lot of practice at secret-keeping. That said, I was still tragically terrible at it. Truth is, some of us are better at keeping secrets than others. But none of us are meant to keep them bottled up inside.

My secrets leaked all over the place — thanks to Mom's incredible intuition, combined with my immense clumsiness when it came to handling them. They bubbled and boiled inside me, making me so uncomfortable I'd lose my brain to bumbling.

One afternoon I haphazardly left a letter from Alan on the entryway table, mixed in with the day's mail as if begging Mom to discover it. Which, of course, she did.

"I'm sorry it didn't work for you to get high last night," he had written. "Next time we should give the bong a try."

After a lot of drama and many tears, a mortifying meeting was called between his parents and mine.

During one of my breakups with Alan, he returned all of my photos, including one he'd recently taken of me in his bathroom. I was dressed in a skimpy red-striped dress, my permed hair wet. On the back I'd written, "Remember this picture, right after our steamy shower together?"

Mom found the picture — which I'd blatantly left on the kitchen counter amidst a stack of homework and other public papers. But this time, she didn't force any apologies. No family-to-family meetings were called. Instead, Mom spent the evening in her room, crying. The muffled sound of her sobs carried me back to kindergarten.

I'd hurt and disappointed her … just as before. I couldn't help making the leap that she cried because I was turning into my birth mom. By the lack of mention of her, I sensed my family had judged my birth mom and the premarital sex she'd had as promiscuous, "bad." I never wanted to feel that shame, that responsibility for Mom's feelings, again.

And yet, I still had a lot of growing up to do.

Even though I felt like a hot mess on the inside, according to outward social measures I'd emerged from childhood to adolescence fairly well. I had strong grades and while no Hermione Granger, was usually among the teachers' favorites. I didn't run with the wild popular crowd, and I wasn't in the lower half of the social rung, either. Every university I applied to accepted me into their programs; a couple offered scholarships.

But I made my share of mistakes along the way to becoming my own person … and how frustrating it was to be so inept at keeping the missteps from Mom, who always seemed on to me! I simultaneously vowed to become the daughter she wanted me to be, and to get better at hiding the darker parts of myself I knew wouldn't live up to her expectations. Years later, in my early twenties when I got pregnant and had an abortion, there was no way I could talk with Mom, even though Mom was the person I needed and wanted to talk with the most.

Ironically, she'd called that day, only minutes after I got back to my first apartment, just a few miles from my parents' home.

"Why aren't you at work?" Mom asked before even saying hello.

"I called in sick," I said. The truth, from a technical perspective. But it was still a lie.

"What's wrong?" I could hear the worry in her voice. Panic, almost—which in turn made me panic. Anything I stammered to say would surely give me away. My tone was anything but okay.

"Why are you calling me at home on a weekday, anyway?" I asked.

"I was going to leave you a message," she said.

"Oh."

I got off the phone as fast as I could. Neither of us mentioned the day again, even though I often wondered what it was all about—whether it was Mom's almost frightening sixth sense—or if it was just a coincidence my guilty conscience made more of than reality demanded.

Several times I wanted to ask Mom. But it would have required sharing my secret. The longing was there, but the opportunity was not. Or so I told myself.

All my life, Mom was the person I wanted to share things with, and the person I needed to know me. ALL of me. And to accept and understand all of me, too—the good and the bad, light and dark. Otherwise, it would hurt too much.

Therein lay the disconnect.

I didn't trust that I would have been wholly accepted. Hadn't I already seen enough evidence, starting in that Safeway parking lot? Hadn't I already experienced first-hand how tricky mothers could be, how they vanish when you least expect it? Instead of risking more wounds to my sensitive heart, I kept working at being a secret keeper.

Over the years, the culmination of my secrets began to divide me from Mom. We laughed together. We vacationed together. We decorated our homes together. We excitedly planned my wedding together. We talked on the phone—a lot. We griped about our husbands together. We were close in many, many ways. But there was always an unspoken sense that something between us was off. Something was missing. My heart.

CHAPTER SEVEN

Chrysalis Crisis

The heart is hopelessly dark and deceitful, a puzzle that no one can figure out.
—Jeremiah 17:9 (MSG)

One day while at my new marketing job in Seattle, a co-worker named Gary approached me at my desk. I didn't know him well, and always thought of him as a gruffy sort. So it surprised me when he knocked on my cubicle wall.

"Uh, hi. Can you scan a photo for me?"

"Yeah, sure." I took the picture as he handed it to me.

"Pretty." I tried to break the awkwardness between us by studying the wedding photo for a conversation cue. "Who are these people?"

"Well, up until Monday I had no idea who these people even were," Gary said.

"Oh." His cryptic response wasn't giving me a lot to work with, and I didn't want to meddle. I lifted up the cover of the scanner, about to place it facedown.

"That woman in the middle is my mother." Gary paused, as if waiting for me to inquire further … and yet in his eagerness he didn't give me the chance. "I just found her you know."

My eyes bugged out. I tried to contain a yelp.

"Oh, really?" I asked, as cool about it as I could, even though the turbulence I felt inside anticipated exactly what he'd say next. *We are alike, Gary and me.*

"I'm adopted." He shrugged, clearly trying to seem unflappable, too.

"That's cool. I am, too." I selected "300 dpi" and hit "scan," while Gary proceeded to describe a one-year escapade searching for his birth mother. Finally, after a mere $300 and an emotionally excruciating wait, an agency found his sixty-year-old birth mother living in Florida. She was given a form letter. The son she gave up forty years ago was searching for her. If she were open to the idea, he'd contact her by phone.

She agreed.

"So I came home from work Monday and just called her," Gary said. "My wife was more nervous than I was. She guzzled the beer she'd pulled out of the fridge that was supposed to calm *me* down."

Gary was still trying to act as nonchalant as I was trying to be, but we were both failing. His fingers fidgeted with the Sharpie in his hand. Nervously, I kept repeating, "Wow, oh wow," after each sentence he uttered.

The more Gary spoke, the more I felt warm blood speeding toward my heart, fast. The thought of looking up my own birth mother began enticing me. *Could I do this someday, too? Would I?*

"Wow, a letter, huh?" I asked. "What if she'd simply said, 'No?'" I shook my head at the thought. "If that's not the ultimate rejection, I don't know what is."

"Oh, it happens all the time," Gary answered. "Believe me, that's kept me up at night for the last several weeks."

I took a pack of mint gum (after kindergarten I stayed away from grape) from my desk drawer. "Would you like a piece?"

Gary shook his head, continuing. "Or here's one: What if she was a prostitute or something, who's given up several kids along the way? You just never know. And then are you supposed to support this pathetic person now that you know she's your mother?"

"Wow," I said again. *Yuck.* These kinds of thoughts had never crossed my mind. Despite Gary's success, he was pecking at the chrysalis I'd wrapped myself up in. I quite liked my chrysalis.

As a teenager, in retaliation for Mom grounding me, I'd often lash out in frustration, "I hate you! I'm going to go find my *real* mom." Most times, the parental power instantly washed from Mom's face and turned into sheer, utter hurt. She clammed up and walked away, and I heard muffled sobs through her door for the rest of the night.

To relieve my guilt and stave off my own tears, I'd lock myself in my room and fantasize about running away to a cooler, younger, hipper mom. One who wouldn't ground me, for starters. Besides hearing that my birth mother was fifteen when I was born, I'd never known much about her. But that was all I needed to get my brain whirling.

Well … that, and a little fuel for my creative mirage.

One day as I sulked in my room listening to a cranked-up radio, the D.J. announced that Madonna was celebrating her thirtieth birthday.

A chrysalis began to weave around me. *Madonna's thirty? I'm fifteen.* I swept the wetness from my cheek and pulled out my calculator, punching in numbers a couple times over, just to be sure I wasn't oversimplifying the math, that I'd gotten it right.

Fifteen years ago Madonna was fifteen. Madonna's my mother! No wonder I listen to her music all the time. It all makes sense now – she was so busy getting her singing career off the ground she didn't have time to be a mom.

As far-fetched as my whimsy was, fantasy attachments are a common byproduct of adoption. "Fantasy attachments are real psychologically. Just as real as anything else. When the child is holding on to their image of what their [birth] mother was or could have been, [the adoptive parent is] standing on the outside. The umbilical cord is still to the mother,"[1] explains child developmental psychologist Dr. Gordon Neufeld. "In transplanting children, the competing attachment is often to the adult least accessible to them."[2]

Madonna as my birth mother certainly wasn't a sustainable fiction. But she came in handy, easily answering that persistent, nagging question in my mind: *Why didn't she keep me?* Madonna lessened the blow of an otherwise implied answer: *I must not be good enough.*

Encased inside my chrysalis I could pretend. It became a protected world where I could play it safe, prove its implied answer wrong. A place to dream.

I could dream about her thinking of me, remembering my birthdays, celebrating them ceremoniously by herself with birthday cakes and candles, writing annual letters to me that she was too afraid to mail.

I could imagine her secretly having found a private detective, who surreptitiously tracked me down and gave her regular progress reports and shot paparazzi-like photos of me from afar, just to make her proud.

When watching an interview with a famous author or athlete I admired, I could romanticize, "That's her." *She's successful, smart, beautiful, athletic, and kind. And I can be just like her someday.*

My birth mom could be as exotic and resplendent as my imagination. Almost as good as reality ... and yet, not quite. Because I couldn't see out of my chrysalis, and could never definitively know whether she measured up to my vision.

"So ... you should think about calling this agency," Gary told me after he'd finished his story and we'd moved onto the subject of me.

"Nah, I don't need to. I've got my family." I blew a bubble to censor myself from saying more. *Besides, I'm nowhere near forty. I've got time.*

I handed Gary his picture back and watched him leave my cubicle.

CHAPTER EIGHT

Love Longing

Keep vigilant watch over your heart; that's where life starts.
—Proverbs 4:23 (MSG)

The first time I held my newborn niece Kenna, it changed me.

Whether or not I shared the same blood as my sister didn't matter. Kenna may as well have been my blood. My family. A precious baby I could call my own.

All right … not exactly "Mine! Mine! Mine!" Kenna belonged to my younger sister Amy—and her high-school-sweetheart-turned-husband, Ryan, of course. But as any sibling knows, the older sister feels a certain sense of ownership when it comes to the younger sibling's treasures. And Kenna was a treasure.

Gone went my resolve not to fawn over babies. Evaporated, the apathy I'd always felt when co-workers toted their newborns into the office, inspiring me to trot off to the restroom or listen to my voicemails. Dissipating, that dogmatic view I'd settled upon after the Columbine High School shootings: never to bring a child into this unsafe, frightening world.

It was more than just my fertility clock ticking away. The wings of my heart had been roused. Kenna never sent me flitting off, looking for an escape. I wanted to fly back to Colorado to see her as much as I could. I wanted to hold Kenna, even rock her. I loved photographing her, with the impossible goal of trying to somehow capture her essence. I caught her first smile on camera as she looked up at

Amy in pure adoration.

I sat with Kenna in the back seat of the car for her first girls' shopping adventure, Mom driving and Amy riding shotgun. I sang to Kenna. I made silly faces, working to make her smile again ... and again. I held out my hand, and marveled at her grip as she squeezed my pinky finger, then eventually fell asleep still clamped on like that. I delighted in the way she put her other hand on her forehead while she slept, while rubbing her wispy hair. I tried to straighten out her head, cocked ever so slightly, ever so uncomfortably in her aunt-facing car seat.

My adoration of Kenna caught me by surprise as much as it caught my family by surprise. C.S. Lewis once wrote, "To love at all is to be vulnerable."[1] Vulnerability was rare for me. Mom and Amy couldn't help but marvel.

One day, while at Mom's house, Amy put Kenna down for a nap in her Pack-n-Play. The second I heard Kenna murmur, I swooped in to rescue my beloved niece. *Babies shouldn't ever have to feel so alone,* my heart said.

Amy frowned, hands on her hips and elbows pointed at her big sister, so blatantly interfering with sleep training. But the smirks from Mom — still a giddy, first-time Grammy — melted Amy's feigned disgust to reveal a mother's pure pride.

I loved watching Amy as a mother. Motherhood had always been Amy's ambition. She was a natural. Our big-sister/little-sister roles had been reversed. Just like that, she seemed the older, wiser sister. She exuded confidence, ease, love. I didn't feel a trace of sibling jealousy — just so totally honored that Amy was letting me get up close to her baby and to be a part of her life. Aunt Sara. I loved my new name.

After the too-short visit to Colorado and Kenna, I had to return to Seattle, where Jeff, our dog Peetey, and my eight-to-six job awaited.

Looking out the airplane window somewhere between Mile High Stadium and Mt. Rainier, I felt a hole in my heart. I missed Kenna so much already, only two hours after we'd shared our goodbyes. I understood for the first time the sadness that swept over my grandma when she'd leave our house after visits, and the tears Mom would always shed after a trip together, her incessant need to get the next one scheduled before the first had even ended. Not that I was a stranger to sadness. But it was a different sadness, this *going-away* sadness. I was much more versed in the *being-left* sadness that turned me numb.

I thought about Kenna throughout the journey back to Seattle, realizing how beholding her face—seeing up close her inherent, radiating goodness—faced me into a possibility: When I was a baby, perhaps I'd had some goodness in me? When Kenna smiled at me I believed she saw it.

Before Kenna was even three months old, she came down with an ear infection. A week on antibiotics didn't help her feel better, so the doctor then diagnosed a respiratory virus.

A few days later, as Amy was on her way to the mountains to meet up with Ryan for a weekend getaway, she heard a voice in her head, "You don't take a child with a respiratory virus up to the mountains."

Even though Amy felt a like a silly, over-reacting mom, she listened to that voice and drove Kenna back to the doctor. Normally, a baby's oxygen saturation should have been over ninety percent, but Kenna's tested at only seventy-eight percent. Kenna was immediately admitted to the hospital and a few days later transferred by ambulance to Children's Hospital Colorado, where a CAT scan showed she had "very diseased lungs." Eventually the doctors diagnosed Kenna with interstitial lung disease (ILD)—extremely rare, especially in babies.

The coincidence was too much for my mother, who had known for about ten years that she also had interstitial lung disease, the result of her autoimmune disease, polymyositis.

"It's not the same kind," Mom said, defensively. "It's totally different from what I have."

It hadn't even occurred to me to make a connection. But after she'd said it, WebMD confirmed that Mom was right. Interstitial lung disease was different in children than adults. At the same time, though, I wondered. Mom's grandmother had lived in a wheelchair for most of her adult life. Was a gene that perhaps skipped generations somehow responsible?

None of that really mattered though to anyone but Mom, who kept mentioning, guilt lacing her words, that it wasn't the same, that she didn't give this to Kenna.

"You can't worry about that, Mom," I'd said on the phone at least a couple of times. "You aren't responsible for the genes you got. Even if it is something in the genes, it's not you giving them."

"It's not the same disease," she said again.

"I know."

Kenna, revealing goodness in me, exposed fragility in my mother.

Kenna spent the next five months at Children's Hospital, undergoing test after test, procedure after procedure, false hope after false hope. Prayers poured out from friends scattered all over the country, across all of our lives. Amy and Ryan started a CaringBridge website, sharing regular updates and scripture passages that helped them make it through each day.

Kenna's first Halloween, her first Thanksgiving, and Amy's thirtieth birthday passed. Christmas passed. Just when it looked like Kenna might have a hope to return home, Valentine's Day was overshadowed by a surgery — putting in a tracheotomy, in hopes that oxygen coming in through Kenna's throat would help her get more air than the nasal canula could.

All that time, Amy only left the hospital once or twice, and Mom stayed there for much of the time, too.

Mom stopped eating. Feeling responsible for the suffering of both her daughter and granddaughter was too much, even without the commonality of the diseased lungs weighing her down with guilt. During Kenna's tracheotomy surgery, as we sat in the waiting room, all of us together, I overheard Mom sobbing to God. "Please, whatever you do, take me. Don't take Kenna. I'm the one who should be going." A worried friend told me Mom had been imploring God for the life trade for a while.

Shortly after Valentine's Day, as Kenna approached eight months old, it was time for Hospice to get involved. Kenna would not be leaving the hospital. She wasn't getting any better, and in fact, without enough air to survive on, was quite uncomfortable. She required the maximum amount of support that modern medicine could provide and still, her oxygen needs couldn't be met. The doctors and nurses, who had become dear friends, said they were approaching a point where they had done all that they could do to help Kenna.

On the CaringBridge page, Amy wrote:

> After a lot of agonizing and praying, we have decided to transfer Kenna to hospice, or "comfort care" on Wednesday. Let me explain what that means: we will be transferring her to her home vent. This vent is not as efficient at keeping her ventilated, so her CO_2 (the blood gas that has been a problem in the past) will slowly rise, which will make her sleepy, and at some point, she just won't wake up. The most important thing will be to keep her totally comfortable.
>
> So, the plan as we see it now, is on Wednesday, we will load her up in her kid cart, hook up the home vent, and take her for a walk outside. Then we

will go directly to the third floor. At that time we will have our pastor, Harvey, come in to dedicate Kenna to God. Then, we will just enjoy every second we can with her. It could be a few hours, or a few days.

This evening we had a photographer here. We got some great pictures of Kenna that we will cherish for the rest of our lives. It was also a great family time with both of our families.

This will probably be the last update for a little while. We are really going to focus on enjoying the moments we have left. We ask for continued prayers for Kenna's comfort, and strength and endurance for Ryan, myself, and our families.

I joined Amy and family as we all said goodbye to Kenna. Without question, it was the most heart-wrenching experience of my life. I will never forget the pain on Amy's and Ryan's faces — nor their bravery, as they resolved to be a source of strength, comfort, and love for Kenna as she took her last breaths in their arms.

At that moment, Mom began to choke. Worried her reaction might be too much for Kenna, and for Amy and Ryan, I accompanied Mom to the bathroom in the hospital suite, where she wailed. "I'm going to throw up," she said. "I'm going to throw up." Her first granddaughter was dying only twelve feet away. Her youngest daughter, still a baby to her, was in tremendous emotional pain. It really was too much, I agreed, but we had to stay grounded for Kenna.

Somehow, through the intense grief, there was intimacy and immeasurable love in wailing and crying together. Love like I'd never known before, sending out this innocent, good baby. I had to believe we were giving her to God until we could meet her again.

A moment of pure love. Perfect love that marked my heart, unguarded, with a longing for more.

CHAPTER NINE

Hatchings

In his hand is the life of every living thing and the breath of all mankind.
—Job 12:10 (ESV)

The shrimp ceviche in Nicaragua was killer. I devoured it—even finished off Jeff's—before slurping up the leftover juice.

Jeff and I had gone out for a late dinner, trying to stay awake long enough to make the turtle-hatching excursion that departed at midnight. Any other night, staying up so late would have been a challenge. We weren't in our fresh twenties anymore! Luckily, I wasn't running on ceviche juice alone. Ecstatic energy fueled me, consuming me with thoughts of the baby turtles we'd soon see. As soon as we'd chosen Nicaragua as our travel destination, the animals, especially the turtles, had appealed to me the most. I was overjoyed that we'd found a way to see them. Given the rain that had recently pounded down on the region, along with extremely poor road conditions, we lucked into finding one tour operator in town who agreed to brave the roads and take us, with another couple, out to the nesting beach.

Midway through the long, bumpy trip to the turtle beach, as we bounced on wooden seats and held on to the rails in front of us, all that shrimp ceviche came back up. I leaned into the pitch of night, out the open-air truck, and vomited all over the outskirts of San Juan del Sur.

The truck driver stopped and walked to the back, sizing me up to see if I was one of those drunk, spring-break-partying *chicas*. Oh, I had been once, but those days were long behind me. Besides, it was Christmas break.

Jeff, speaking absolutely no Spanish but shockingly fluent in gesturing the words "bumpy" and "very sick," apologized on my behalf while I threw up some more. The driver decided not to boot us into the remote wooded area of Nowhere, Nicaragua, and an hour later I stumbled out of the truck—exhausted and yet equally elated. This was such an important part of this vacation. No rotten ceviche could stop me.

I gripped my stomach as our group checked in with the Sandinista guards who sat around a table, machine guns hanging off their belts, hand guns lying next to their poker chips and straight flushes. I flushed, wondering if they'd shoot me if I started hurling on their feet.

"Are you sure you're still up for this?" Jeff whispered as we descended the stairs outside the office. "We could wait in the truck."

"I'm not missing this! No way." I flapped my hand, so Jeff and the other couple in our group could go ahead while I threw up one more time in the privacy of the bushes that flanked the path to the beach.

"Sara, get over here! You've got to see this!" Jeff called out as I stood. Dizzy, I made my way toward the tiny flashlight he shone on the ground in front of me. "Watch your step, though. They're everywhere!"

I looked down, and sure enough, dozens of teeny turtles waddled right at my feet, having emerged from their sandy nest only a few feet away. I watched the trail of them, struck by their determination as they army-crawled over the sand toward the ocean, even though their eyes were barely open and they were surely dizzy, too.

The truck driver I'd somehow endeared myself to came over to show me the baby turtle in his hand. "Pick it up. It's okay to hold it."

"Really?" I asked. "But won't I hurt it?"

"No." He smiled, opening up my hand, gingerly placing the turtle in my palm. "It's okay."

I knew better. Somewhat of an animal activist, I knew we shouldn't have been shining flashlights, taking flash pictures, holding these vulnerable creatures, disrupting nature. And yet ... here, irresistibly in my hand, was this turtle — this little turtle with slits for eyes and a straight, tiny line for a mouth. Its miniature grey shell, covered in hexagons, was still peppered with sand.

In a way, it was like holding Kenna, or my childhood butterfly friend. Perhaps, even, my aborted child — a flash of a thought, hardly perceptible. I marveled at this perfect, innocent, beautiful baby turtle right in my grasp. I felt its slow-and-steady, tenacious spirit course through me. I stared in awe at its flippers, almost winglike, as they kept rotating, paddling, pushing against my hand. There was such a sense of magic to it all that I half expected the turtle to lift off and carry onward to the water through the air. I couldn't help but wonder at God's impeccable, complex design. How does this brand-new turtle know exactly what to do, where to go? I rarely prayed, but an invocation seemed important to ensure I hadn't disrupted the turtle from its journey, that it would make it, in spite of me. *Just let me relish this one beautiful moment. Please say I'm not destroying this precious creature.*

Carefully, I placed the turtle back on the sand, facing the water. In case my prayer hadn't been enough, I blew the turtle a kiss for good luck and watched it lumber on its journey until it disappeared into the crashing black waves. I tiptoed across the sand, avoiding the puddles of other turtles still clambering up from other nests, before making my own journey ... back to the bushes to barf some more.

After Nicaragua Jeff and I flew to Naples, Florida, to visit my parents for Christmas and then celebrate Mom's sixtieth on December 26th. For this milestone birthday, I treated Mom to a mother-daughter spa day at the Naples Beach Hotel. But the best present I could give her wasn't to hatch until later.

Freshly massaged and relaxed, we were about to head across the street for lunch at the hotel's beach-side restaurant—Mom's favorite spot in all of Naples. Before we left the spa, though, I stopped.

"Hold on, Mom. I'd better use the bathroom one more time before we leave."

"There's a restroom across the street," she offered. "It might be faster."

"I'll be quick." I bolted, no time to discuss the matter further.

At the beach, I picked at my salad. It really didn't appeal. The ceviche had played quite a toll on my appetite—it'd been almost a week since the night I'd eaten it in Nicaragua, but my stomach still couldn't shake its memory.

We left the restaurant to head back home, stopping along the way at the natural food grocery store—the one Mom always took me to for the "weird food" Jeff and I liked. Mom had given up on stocking food for us, but whenever we arrived for a visit, she'd bring me to Wynn's Market so I could pick out all the organic comfort food we were used to in Seattle. This time, Mom and I also needed to buy food for our upcoming sailing trip—a three-day adventure along Southwestern Florida's intercostal waterways to Sanibel Island. We'd be leaving the next day, together with Dad and Jeff, as soon as the tide came back in.

Mom and I split up in the store, as was our custom, to scout out the groceries we each liked. Usually I loved this store, with its beautiful food displays and mix of both familiar and unique organic foods. But that day, I found it unusually … disgusting. Nothing smelled right. The deli made me gag. I plugged my nose as I walked by the gourmet olives. The seafood section? I couldn't bear to look its way. Shrimp, and possibly all seafood, would forever remain in my past.

I'd just stepped out of the bathroom hallway when Mom found me, her cart brimming with food. She looked at the basket hanging from my elbow, a measly box of crackers lying lonely inside, as if in grocery jail.

She smiled. "Sara! What have you been doing all this time?"

"I can't find anything that looks good." I felt like a child, grumpy at my mom for bringing me to this horrible place. "Can we just go?"

Mom put the convertible top down as we drove out of the Wynn's parking lot and onto the Tamiami Trail. I downgraded from child to dog, leaning my head out the car to slurp up air, hoping to cleanse my tainted nostrils.

"Um … do you think you could be pregnant?" Mom asked as we approached the stoplight.

"No." I laughed. "You don't understand, Mom. That ceviche was really awful. I'll never eat it again."

"Hmmm."

The next morning, it was time to leave for our sailing trip. Jeff carted our duffel bags and groceries from the house to the boat while Dad worked on the engine. Me? Back in bed, after the sight of scrambled eggs, along with the remnants of their cracked shells sitting in a bowl on the counter, sent me bolting from the kitchen.

"I've got to run to the store for a couple more quick things," Mom announced. "Do you want to come?"

"What are you getting?"

"Sunscreen." She twirled the car keys. "And, would you like me to pick up a pregnancy test, too? What do you think?"

"Those tests are super expensive, Mom. I'd hate for you to waste your money."

"Oh, I don't mind. How much can they cost?"

"I think they're like, thirty dollars or something," I said.

"I'll only get one." Mom grinned.

Her enthusiasm was infectious. I smirked back. "Okay. Yeah, sure … just in case."

Mom dashed toward the garage door. "I won't be long," she sang out.

I couldn't help but laugh — at her excitement, and out of nervousness. It was weird, having Mom help me buy a pregnancy test. I'd never admitted to having sex, even if Jeff and I had been married for over four years now. Another secret between Mom and me.

I thought about Amy, in Colorado right then with Ryan and their healthy newborn baby, Evan, only a few months old. As sisters, we always unconsciously chose each other's opposites. I liked sushi. She liked beef. I gravitated toward solo sports. She played team sports. I drank wine. Amy … Diet Pepsi. Tomato. Tomah-to. Mother. Un-mother. Even entertaining the thought of motherhood felt like a violation of our sisterly social code, our uniqueness as separate people.

Twenty minutes later, Mom had returned and I was leaning over the bathroom counter, studying the test stick.

"Jeff?" I yelled.

Mom, just around the corner, called out. "You okay?"

"Uh … yeah. Can you get Jeff?"

"Of course!" Mom said. "Jeff! Sara needs you."

Jeff, sweaty from all the trips back and forth from house to sailboat, joined me in the bathroom.

"What's going on?" he asked.

"Shut the door," I said, pointing at the pink and white test stick that looked like one of Smurfette's skis. "Look!"

We stared at the stick. Printed right on it, the words: Two lines: pregnant. One line: not pregnant. For a minute we studied the very distinct, pink lines—two of them. Jeff smiled. I smiled. "What does this mean?" he asked, tearing up.

"Uh ... I don't know."

We checked the stick again, in case the results had changed when we'd looked away from the stick and into each other's eyes.

"Should I get your mom?" Jeff asked after our embrace.

I nodded slowly, a bit dazed. Jeff and I hadn't been officially "trying." But, ever since I'd fallen in love with Kenna we weren't exactly not trying, either, which was pretty much trying, but just not admitting it. The cautious route. This was good news, but I was scared. *Yes, I did want my mom.*

Jeff slid open the pocket door of the bathroom. "Linda? Linda, can you come here?"

"Yes?" Mom practically ran into me as I stepped out of the bathroom to meet her.

I held up the stick. "You were right, Mom!"

"Oh, Sara! Oh, Sara!" She hugged me, placed her hands on her chest, then heaved as if she'd been holding her breath all morning long. "Really? Really?"

"I guess so!" I giggled. Jeff, standing beside me, giggled, too.

Mom showed me her shaky hands, wiped her instantly perspiring forehead. "Oh, Sara! You're going to have a baby! You guys are pregnant! Who would have thought? The spa was nice, but this? Wow!"

And so I had hatched Mom's very best birthday present.

A real "hatching" would come later. A real parent would have to emerge with the baby, too. With turtle mothers, the job is done once the eggs are buried in the sand. But I was no turtle. Questions full of self-doubt already started gnawing at me. *Was this responsible of me, of us, to bring a child into this messed-up world? Was I up for this, for motherhood?* I'd never thought of myself as "motherhood material." *What if I couldn't find the mother in me, and totally screwed up my child?*

Mom's pure and expressive joy, though, lifted away my fears and doubts, enabling me to wonder at the enchantment of it all—to marvel at the possibilities of love, life, and motherhood.

CHAPTER TEN

The Mysteries of Look-Alikes

Apparently some people have been introducing fantasy stories and fanciful family trees that digress into silliness instead of pulling the people back into the center, deepening faith and obedience.
—1 Timothy 1:4 (MSG)

"Wow. Your baby looks *nothing* like you," an acquaintance named Samantha said to me in passing. "She must look like your husband."

I don't believe Samantha meant for the comment to sting, but it burned and festered under my skin for weeks.

While she'd been the most direct, Samantha wasn't the only one who'd proclaimed this. Ever since Violet was born, friends, family, and strangers seemed to delight in the game of studying my infant daughter to tell me she looked more like Jeff than me. Or, more than once or thrice, I'd be an omission altogether: "My goodness, she looks *exactly* like Jeff, doesn't she?"

They acted like it was a pop quiz, or a mystery, I'd asked them to solve—nodding in earnest and donning a clownish grin, waiting for me to confirm they'd indeed cracked the case—only I hadn't asked them to solve anything. It was a mystery, but one I was still trying to solve on my own. I didn't want anyone telling me the answer ... especially the wrong answer.

It wasn't a paternity issue, but if I hadn't birthed Violet myself for twenty-six epic hours, I might have demanded a maternity test. And obviously I found Jeff plenty attractive. I had fallen in love with his looks just as much as his beautiful being. It wouldn't be so tragic if Violet indeed looked like Jeff.

But as an adoptee, I'd never had the luxury of my own genes to look at—a luxury non-adoptees can take for granted. I had no blood relatives to compare myself to—to figure out where my dimples came from ... to find out who gave me what my Papa called my "Milwaukee Front" toddler's Buddha belly ... to know whether my sometimes quirky outlook was a matter of nature or if it was all nurture ... and, to understand if I'd inherited my brokenness. *Maybe my genes were what was wrong with me. Maybe that explained me.*

Violet was my inaugural window into my genes. I couldn't help it. Studying the first traces of my genes through my baby girl—the very first blood relative I'd ever known—was a mystery I couldn't seem to turn away from.

Growing up, whenever people asked, I'd always say that I was a cross between a Swede and a German. My revered Papa was Swedish, after all. We ate Grandma's Swedish meatballs and buttered *lefse* and (gag) lutefisk every Christmas Eve. Dad, who was in the process of publishing a book about my great-great grandfather Lewis Easterly, had written that the Easterlys originally hailed from Germany, the Netherlands, Poland, and England. I could have easily passed as from any of those places, I thought.

Looks seemed to confirm these wonderings. Both Germans and Swedes came with freckles and blonde hair, didn't they? People used to think my cousin Jenny and I should star in those old Doublemint Gum commercials featuring twins. I also looked a lot like Mom with her Swedish roots. Just as people commented to me as a new mother, they'd comment to Mom and me about our shared looks. Well into my adulthood, friends, family, and strangers would rave to Mom about how much she and I looked alike. "It's so obvious you are mother and daughter," they'd tell us. "Your dancing eyes ... they match!" Mom loved the guessing game, never revealing that I was adopted, proudly smiling along. I liked it, too … even though their comments were always a brittle reminder that I couldn't truly claim the heritage or looks of my adoptive family. I knew it was a pretending game. I knew none of them had accurately solved the mystery — the mystery of where I came from.

But then, after a brief meconium inhalation scare in the hospital, Jeff whisked our newborn daughter, Violet, over to me. As she nursed in my arms that night — and every day and night after that for the next six months until I got pregnant again — I had all the time in the world to marvel at Violet's peach fuzz, so blonde it was almost white. *She really could be Swedish,* I thought, *or German. Maybe that actually is where I, now we, came from. How ironic would that be, to have guessed right? To have been raised right?*

When I pulled out the baby albums Mom made for me, I'd analyze the pictures. I'd always cherished the photo of Dad and me when I was just a few weeks new — Dad sound asleep on the couch while I slept in a ball, secure on his chest. I loved the Polaroid of Mom's sister and best friend, my Aunt Carol, giving me one of my first baths. I especially relished the picture of me as a ten-month-old in the country club grass — flanked on either side by Grandma, praying, and Mom, smoking. Front and center I stood, ready to conquer the world in my yellow terrycloth swimsuit that matched Mom's sunshine yellow bikini. With full access to Violet, I looked for opportunities to recreate those images. I skipped the praying and the smoking, looking to stage the same scenarios with my little baby model — capturing similar moments on camera myself, then setting the generational pictures side by side to study at length.

The photos looked a lot alike. *We* looked a lot alike. Whether anyone else said so or not, I could see myself in her.

And yet, I could also see that Violet was different. She wasn't me.

She wasn't Jeff, either.

She wasn't adopted.

And I was so glad. She hadn't been abandoned. She'd never be abandoned—I'd make sure of that. *That's* what was different.

But just as it had been when I'd held Kenna, I'd sensed something. A whisper of a something, too soft to fully detect. Maybe, like my darling baby girl, there was preciousness in me, too.

It remained a mystery. A mystery I had yet to solve.

CHAPTER ELEVEN

Lofty Ideals

"Martha, Martha, you are anxious and troubled about many
things, but one thing is necessary."
—Luke 10:41 (ESV)

My two daughters napped while I chatted on the phone with Mom.
It'd been a while since we'd talked—almost a week, I think. I didn't
like being on the phone with anyone, not even my own mother, while
my daughters were awake. *What kind of message did that send to my
babies? That they didn't matter?* Problem was, it was hard to squeeze
in conversations with all the people I wanted to talk to, and accom-
plish all the things I wanted to get done—like write, run loads of
laundry, puree baby food—during the rare daytime hours when both
girls' sleep schedules synced. Mom, though, still took top priority ...
especially when I wanted her help, or needed a sympathetic ear for
my gripes.

With my "two under two," lack of sleep was the topic of the year
for me, and so I grumbled about it to Mom.

"Violet won't stay in her bed," I complained. "Last night we
probably spent two hours going back and forth from our room to
hers. So infuriating!"

"You wouldn't stay in your bed, either," Mom said, chuckling.

"So what'd you do?"

"That's why we had to lock the door to our bedroom."

"Huh?" I asked.

"So you wouldn't come into our room and climb into our bed."

"Oh … well, we don't have locks on our—"

"We'd wake up in the morning to find you curled up outside the door, sleeping on the floor against our door."

"Really?" I sort of half-laughed with her. A nervous laugh, though, as I thought of my vulnerable little toddler self, not that different from Violet's tender age of eighteen months, all alone like that. I shivered, thinking about how cold I must have been, my bare legs exposed by my thin polyester Bambi nightgown.

"Yup. Sound asleep on the floor. We'd find you there almost every morning." Mom laughed again, the apparent hilarity of it all.

"Huh." *Well that explains a few things*, I thought, my mind a flurry with newly reframed memories of my profound childhood fears of being alone, of the dark, of being the last person in the house to fall asleep.

After we hung up, I wondered whether I could ever do such a thing to my daughters. *Absolutely not! What kind of mother could?* I thought again of my little girl self and almost cried. I would have, too, if I hadn't been seething so much over Mom's flippant parenting stories and shoddy advice … and if my daughters hadn't cried out just then. Nap-time, mama-time over.

Thankfully, having two children just fifteen months apart meant I spent countless hours nursing—and reading—while pinned to a comfy, soft rocking chair patterned with beautiful swirls, a shower gift from Mom that perfectly coordinated with the nursery's Springhill Green walls. I logged many, many hours in that chair over the course of a couple of years, usually with a baby held horizontal and a book held upright—at least until burping time.

I wasn't merely reading, though. There was no time for "merely reading." In those important hours of breastfeeding and bonding with my daughters, I was also giving myself a crash course in parenting. I didn't say so to the mother who bought the very chair I rocked and read in, but I planned to be a different breed of mother. Unlike her—a mother who left her child sleeping alone on the floor all night—I would get it right. Just as I'd catalogued my stuffies, I had catalogued each and every one of Mom's faults—the hurtful things she'd said, the ways she failed me, the ways she hadn't seen me, the ways she'd dismissed me. I vowed to be different. Perfect.

My reading log for this quest included: *The Baby Book* by Dr. William Sears; *Becoming Attached* by Robert Karen; T. Berry Brazelton's *Touchpoints: Your Child's Emotional and Behavioral Development*; *Your Child's Growing Mind* by Jane Healy; *Parenting from the Inside Out* by Dan Siegel; *Raising An Emotionally Intelligent Child* and *The Heart of Parenting* by John Gottman; David Elkins's *The Hurried Child*; Alfie Kohn's *Unconditional Parenting*; *Trees Make the Best Mobiles* by Jessica Teich and Brandel France de Bravo; Anne Lamott's memoir *Operating Instructions*; *Happiest Baby on the Block* by Harvey Karp; *The Scientist in the Crib* by Alison Gopnik and Andrew N. Meltzoff; *NurtureShock* by Po Bronson and Ashley Merryman; and *Parenting with Love and Logic* by Foster Cline and Jim Fay.

Never mind my spinning head. Even as my leaning tower of books wobbled, I planned ahead with books like Alfie Kohn's *What to Look for in a Classroom* and *The Schools Our Children Deserve*. My babies would be school-ready in the not-too-distant future, after all. I researched how to keep my daughters safe from sexual predators with *Protecting the Gift* by Gavin de Becker. For good measure, I read up on allowances: *Earn It, Learn It* by Alisa Weinstein. Never too soon to raise a contributing member of society!

When I wasn't reading or burping my babies, I toted them around with me to breastfeeding support groups, a neighborhood new-parent group for couples, and a "Listening Mothers" support group. I subscribed to a slew of parenting blogs and magazines. I sat in on webinars on how and when to talk to kids about sex. My information intake was truly astounding. But onward I searched. Becoming a parent made me feel a huge void inside myself. I'd often told Jeff I wasn't "marriage material" — let alone "motherhood material." But I'd proceeded with both, anyway. More and more knowledge was surely the answer if I wanted to get it all right.

Mom delighted in watching from the sidelines as a grandparent. One day, while in Seattle for a visit, she remarked, "Who would have thought, Sara? You do all these incredible feats for work, run these big events for all these big corporations, and nothing ever flusters you. And here these tiny little babies of yours really have you flummoxed."

"Yeah." I laughed. "I know. It's pretty nuts."

"But you're approaching it just like you do everything else," she said. "All in. You never do anything halfway. That's for sure."

Mom was right. I was all in. But it wasn't purely a rebellion against her ways. The real force of energy came from my feelings of inadequacy. As a mother, I felt so unqualified. My inherent brokenness, the emotional baggage I'd unknowingly been carrying for so much of my life — together with the newly conscious view into my own childhood and way I had been parented — seemed to be screaming, almost as loud as my babies did, for attention.

Rather than bear the pain, I resolved to overcome it all through my lofty ideals. I had to be different — yes, from my mother, but mostly from myself.

Advice to a Too-Busy Mama

By Linda Easterly, to Sara

1. Start day with yogurt and cereal—real easy.

2. Sing while you run errands ... probably kiddy songs.

3. Tell another mommy that she looks pretty.

4. Do a drive-up for lunch. Stay out of the kitchen; it takes too much time.

5. During nap-time don't take any personal calls, even from your own Mom.

6. Make yourself say, "That is good enough," and move on.

7. Put a large box of blocks in the middle of floor and tell Violet she has to play by herself today. A bit of ignoring is good for a kid.

8. Have an enjoyable dinner when you just eat and not try to multi-task.

9. Tell four people, "No, I can't do it. I'm too busy right now."

10. Soak in a 20-minute bath, remembering your favorite vacation. Dry off and use a special lotion to treat your skin.

11. Tall glass of wine is in order now.

12. At 10:30, pat yourself on the back, recognizing all that you accomplished today and put your head on a satin pillow, thanking God that you are you, and remembering that your mommy loves you.

CHAPTER TWELVE

Purpose in the Potential

Consider it a sheer gift, friends, when tests and challenges come at you from all sides.
—James 1:2 (MSG)

While canvassing a neighborhood moms' forum one day, a post caught my eye, advertising a presentation called "Making Sense of Young Children." One of the bullet points promised insights into "how to respond effectively to aggression."

Violet had been growing increasingly aggressive—doing what is best described as cow-tipping, only with her newly sitting sister, all of three months new. Naturally, I blamed myself ... and quickly signed up for the workshop, confident that I'd find behavioral guidance to get me through this next phase of parenting my "two under two."

The presenter, Rebeca, based her talk on the work of Dr. Gordon Neufeld, a developmental psychologist from Vancouver, British Columbia, and the author of *Hold On to Your Kids*—surprisingly, a book I'd not yet discovered. Rebeca described his attachment-based approach, saying, "It's about attachments beyond just what we think of as attachment with small babies." She spoke about the different stages that babies—and all of us—go through to attach to one another, from the more superficial levels of being near each other, to the deeper levels of love and then to being truly known. She talked about the power of relationship—how a child will want to be good for those she's attached to—emphasizing the importance of having your child's heart.

I fervently scribbled notes on nearly every word Rebeca shared, worried I'd forget this language, these words and theories that were equally unfamiliar and yet so simple, so natural. I'd never articulated my desired approach to raising my daughters, but pretty much everything Rebeca said felt spot on. The words she used also gave me a lens to look through my own childhood. Describing time-outs and consequences, she said, "While it may work, it makes caring unsafe. The child says, 'Caring sets me up for getting hurt, so I'm going to resist going too deep.'" Later, she added, "But when we lose our caring, we're no longer humane. It's what gets us stuck in our attachment growth."

In my heart, without needing to ponder for long, I immediately knew these things to be true.

After years upon years of hurts and heartaches, breakups, letdowns, life had strengthened my resolve to live out my personal motto, stolen from a line in the movie *Nadia*: "I'm not crying. I never cry."

Nobody did see me cry ... or express my fears or deepest dreams. It was easier to blame the dark, horrible world than to make space for the true longings of my heart—and the ensuing disappointments that might befall me should I allow them to soar. After my loud protests against having children, even Jeff still believed I'd never wanted them—even after I'd birthed our two daughters. For our wedding, I'd insisted on a no-kids policy for our guests. Though I'd fallen in mad love with Violet and Olive as soon as they entered the world, sometimes I snuck off and hid when Jeff brought them to me, insisting, once again, that the only way to soothe their cries was through my breasts. In these ways Jeff saw me at my worst—feeling used and struggling with resentment—neither of us pondering whether it might have something to do with my adoption.

And yet, having children had been a huge dream for me. As a young girl, I loved tearing out pictures from magazines of kid models that looked like me to create mock family photo albums, naming the four children I planned to have after V.C. Andrews's characters.

But I never shared any of that with Jeff. He bought my stories of disinterest. But was my hardened, pretend-not-to-care façade really working?

I didn't have time to reflect further. Rebeca talked too fast. So I just kept transcribing her every word.

Not only did the presentation content resonate, but I'd also been touched by Rebeca's soft, feminine-yet-strong presence. She wasn't afraid of revealing her vulnerability, and yet it didn't undo her confidence and command of the room. She used heart language I hadn't come across in any parenting books or advice doled out by Mom and Amy, my closest veteran parents—like "adding in the caring rather than taking something away," and "giving our children an invitation to exist in our company just as they are," and "making it safe for our children to depend on us."

Rebeca saw not only children, but moms, too, with empathy. "Don't feel guilty for what you didn't know until now. Children need us to have confidence. Don't beat yourself up. Just get to work," she said. As she described situations with her own children and shared her kind, thoughtful, and unconventional responses, I marveled at the wisdom, gentleness, and power in that approach.

Later that day, as I transferred my scrawls into seventeen typed pages of Times New Roman font-size 10, I decided to put my faith in what Rebeca described as Nature's plan. Her talk was not about religion. But for the first time in a long time—perhaps since watching the baby turtles in Nicaragua—it made me ponder God. *Of course,*

God designed the messy and often frustrating phases of childhood with great purpose. I wanted to understand that design ... and learn how to support it.

I felt lovestruck—by so much more than the minutia of a toddler's infant-tipping and what I could do to snuff out that "delinquent" behavior—but with the possibility of offering my children something so much greater and more important: a path for becoming fully mature as human beings. Maybe in the process, I could get there, too.

CHAPTER THIRTEEN

Lung Wings

But those who wait upon God get fresh strength. They spread
their wings and soar like eagles. They run and don't get tired, they
walk and don't lag behind.
—Isaiah 40:31 (MSG)

Mom's youngest granddaughter—my youngest daughter Olive—
was only five months old when Mom's polymyositis took its drastic
south-bound turn for the worse. Before that, during the fifteen years
since she'd been diagnosed with the autoimmune disease, I'd been
able to act as though her disease was a gnat—an annoyance, sure
to disappear as long as I swatted it away, pushed it out of my sight.
Even if the gnat still swarmed overhead, it wasn't hovering right in
front of my face, and it tricked me into believing it had flown off and
out of our lives.

Sure, Mom had what the doctors called a "crackling" in her
lungs, and they were constantly running chest x-rays and lung function tests. Eventually, too, she had to breathe with the support of an
oxygen tank at night. Even so, Mom seemed to be fine, reveling in
the retired life she shared with Dad, Aunt Carol, and many friends in
Florida—shopping, sailing, shopping, dining, shopping—and traveling to Seattle to see her grandbabies as often as an adoring Grammy
could.

"Somehow, I seemed to do a pretty good job of ignoring the
whole disease, and became what I call a closet oxygen user, making
sure no one knew the magnitude of my needs," Mom once wrote,
describing her health.

But after a bout of pneumonia, Mom's lungs were unable to pump enough oxygen into her body—even with the help of the various machines and drugs the pulmonologists loaded her up with. Whenever she'd move, even with oxygen support, she would lose air, and so became stuck at home in bed. Words we'd added to our family vocabulary during Kenna's months in the hospital came breezing back into conversations: desatting ... oxygen flow ... chest tube ... lung biopsies. Two different kinds of trach tubes were put into Mom's throat—a more direct route, supposedly, to help the oxygen flow better.

Within a couple of months, Mom's condition had advanced to such a severe point that she was a candidate for a double lung transplant. After weeks of waiting, many days of testing, and over $50,000 in medical bills, finally Mom was placed on The List. Akin to Santa's Naughty-or-Nice list, this one relied on computer algorithms and doctors to play Santa—or rather, God—filling in the names of The Nice who would be saved.

The wait for a new set of lungs could take between two weeks and eighteen months. Mom proved a challenging match since only nine percent of people share her blood type, and the new lungs would need to come from someone 4'10" to 5'3" because hers had scarred and shriveled so much that other organs adjusted accordingly and moved into the open space. She also had antibodies that could create an automatic unacceptability.

We waited, and waited. It didn't seem right that we were waiting for somebody else to die so that Mom would not. But that's what we were doing. In that way, organ transplanting is very much like adoption: an organ is transplanted from a body not fit for life, just as a child is transplanted from a home deemed unfit for growth. One family's loss would be another family's gain.

With each day we waited, it looked as though Mom would die first, anyway, as her health, and breathing, got worse by the day.

Through it all, though, even on the brink of death, Mom kept her faith.

"I have every confidence that God is big enough to handle this problem!" she wrote on the CaringBridge page we maintained to keep friends and family members updated on her condition.

Another time, Mom shared this story:

> My grandson, Evan, has been told he has to hold a hand when crossing the street. So ... typical for Evan, he clutches his own hand for dear life (till it is blue) and says, "I take Effan's hand."
>
> Today in church there was a song about taking the Savior's hand and I could picture me saying "I take Linda's hand" or "I take the doctor's hand" or "I take the drug's hand" ... holding on to each for dear life. So I think I learned a whole lot from my two-year-old "Little Man." I want to try to picture myself taking, confidently and comfortably, my Savior's hand!
>
> Thank you, Effan!

I found Mom's God stories, like this one, kind of cute—in a naïve sort of way. Sometimes, I'd catch hold of a fleeting thought, wondering if Mom's faith was getting in her way of expressing valid important emotions and medical concerns. But mostly I humored her, as I often humored her faith, and didn't say anything. No need to question her beliefs—just as I didn't feel the need to debate people who weren't vegetarians, like me, about their carnivorous eating. *To each her own.* And even though it mostly didn't bother me that she shared her Christianity so outwardly, once in a while I found it annoying how she managed to bring God into just about every conversation.

Still, I cried myself to sleep each night and tried to remember to pray. Real prayers and real tears flowed—for the first time in a long time. I cried for Mom. For me. And possibly mostly for my girls. My daughters were still so young—Olive, in fact, lying next to me in the bed, freshly nursed and swaddled. Thinking about the loss for my children, too young to understand, too young to know and be known by Mom, devastated me the most. *What if my babies grow up without memories of their Grammy?* God had to be there listening. I needed God to be there listening.

But I also knew, despite the thousands of prayers asking for Kenna to live, that God didn't always listen. *Did prayers even matter? Didn't God already know how it would all turn out, anyway? Would one prayer sobbed in my bed, or a thousand written on a CaringBridge site, actually sway God's mind?* I tried to believe the Christian quips: "God has his reasons," or "God sometimes needs to call his angels home." But deep down those explanations seemed lame and anesthetized me when it came to God. I prayed away, though. *Just a little more time, please. Somebody who's going to die, anyway — not because of us.*

On November 4th Mom received the call we had all been praying for, whether our faith was convicted or forced. "Get into the hospital!" the transplant coordinator told Mom. At that very moment, the pulmonologists were flying out to visit the recently deceased donor and check on the state of the lungs that seemed to be an ideal match for Mom, according to the computer. While nurses prepped Mom for surgery, the doctors approved the flawless lungs and flew them back to Tampa General to begin the eight-hour surgery.

Later, Mom wrote:

About 11:00 or 11:30 p.m. I got wheeled in! Everyone was dressed in scrubs, talking with one another. I was basically being ignored, so I had a chance to just look around and realize, to my amazement, that I was calm as could be. I did acknowledge that this could be the first day of my new life or my last day. I had had a long talk with my Lord and I was okay whichever way it went. In heaven I will get to reunite with my grandbaby, Kenna,

*my special dad, and see the face of my Lord. On the other hand, if all went
well, I get to continue with my very special family, which now includes
three grandbabies.*

In less than twenty-four hours off the operating table, Mom's ven-
tilator was removed and she began breathing on her own using her
new lungs. By the time Amy and I had flown in to see her the next
day, Mom was sitting up, eating dinner, and cradling her new iPad
to watch a slideshow of all her grandbabies' photos, cut to Karen
Carpenter's "I'm On Top of the World." The doctors had projected a
three-week hospital stay. Mom, though, was out of the hospital and
back home a mere eleven days later, to the marveling of the nurses
and doctors, who called Mom their "star patient." That same week,
she even made the hospital holiday party thrown for other lung
transplant recipients, all donning glorious smiles under their germ-
containing masks.

One of Mom's friend's remarked, "You are a walking miracle."

"You must feel like a butterfly coming out of its womb," another
commented.

"Answered prayers!" many others chimed in.

I had to agree with their sentiments. Prayers had been answered.

Three weekends later, Mom and I were out shopping the
Thanksgiving weekend sales. When we got back home, I helped my
parents trim the Christmas tree. At the bottom of the tree, underneath
sailboat and seashell ornaments, we placed a lung-shaped pillow—
the one gifted to Mom from hospital volunteers who sewed them for
transplant recipients to cuddle, post-surgery. Patterned in shades of
green, blue, and chartreuse, each color outlined in veiny black lines,
it almost looked like a butterfly. Lung wings.

Dad's Christmas gift for Mom echoed similar inspiration—a sapphire butterfly necklace, symbolizing both the physical shape of her new lungs and her metamorphosis. A rebirth with her second chance at life.

And for Mom, of course, both lung wings served as a reminder of her ever-fruitful faith and a different kind of rebirth ... that all began with my need for a butterfly heaven.

The Big Day

By Linda Easterly

It was on a Thursday,
so warm and so bright
When a call came through
at early light.

First thought, as always,
"Could it be Kim?"
To start my life over —
breathing again?

My gosh it was,
it was really her!
This is the call
I'd been praying for.

They had some lungs
reserved just for me
So hurry to Tampa
as quick as could be.

Bob was off teaching
his sailing class
So, my buddy, Jodi,
I called really fast.

"Jodi, it's time!"
I somehow spat out
"Am I late for coffee?"
she started to shout.

"No, my friend;
this is our day
Tampa just called.
Let's be on our way."

She screamed. I screamed.
We were both quite a mess.
Both of us shaking
and nearly helpless.

So our trip to Tampa
was just so funny
We thought we were lost
and it got rainy, not sunny.

We thought we were totally
all out of gas
And friendship, we agreed,
cannot be surpassed.

By 11 a.m. I was
in gown and mask
"So, when do we do this?"
I excitedly asked.

Well, wouldn't you know?
Ya, sure you do
It was ten hours later
when we left that room.

So, here comes the good part,
the part I just love
About the miracles
sent from above.

God hand-picked a team
to get the job done
And He gave me a beautiful,
healthy new lung
(two, actually, but that doesn't rhyme)

I won't talk about
the next several days
Thankfully much of it
was in a haze.

Be sure as you're sittin' there,
just hear what I say
God let me grow stronger
and healthier each day.

When I open my eyes
and know I can breathe
I thank Him, I love Him,
and say I believe.

He provided these friends,
these nurses, a doctor.
To let me be GRAMMY
a little bit longer.

CHAPTER FOURTEEN

Wingless

Honesty lives confident and carefree, but Shifty is sure to be
exposed.
—Proverbs 10:9 (MSG)

During our next family visit to my parents' house in Florida, less
than a year after her double lung transplant, I discovered that Mom
had changed. First thing in the morning she jumped into the pool to
play with Jeff and the girls. It was her first actual swim with Violet
and Olive, who were newly three and almost two. Before, Mom had
always just enjoyed the kids from the deck. Come to think of it, that's
how it had been for me, too. I couldn't recall her ever joining me in
the pool when I was a child. So it was especially uncharacteristic
when clouds migrated in, pouring rain on all their heads, and Mom
stayed in the pool. She held on to Violet's arms, and the two of them,
unfazed by the deluge, leaned back in the pool with their mouths
agape, lapping up raindrops. I thought about diving in with them,
too, but soaking up the scene, poolside, offered me greater delight.

Eventually Mom dried off and joined me at the table to chart out
plans for our week together. Right away she started talking about
her work at Butterfly House, forgetting she'd told me about it over
the phone at least four times already. The rain had moved up the
coast, but I sensed a disturbance in the air. Jeff and Dad played with
the girls in the hot tub, dipping their chubby legs in the water and
swirling their tiny bodies about. Happy, delighted squeals exploded
around us, and every once in a while we'd get sprayed as warm

water flew our way—in sharp contrast to the trepidation I felt.

"I go there every Wednesday," Mom said. "Would you like to come with me this week? You could bring Olive."

"Sure," I said. "Although ... what time? Her nap schedule—"

"The girls there learn all kinds of practical skills, like how to cook, balance their checking accounts—things to prepare them for their lives as new single mothers—even how to sew buttons onto shirts. You could have used that!"

"Yeah, right," I said, watching Violet bravely leap from the edge of the hot tub and into the pool while Mom told me stories about a couple of her favorite pregnant girls at Butterfly House. It occurred to me I wasn't listening, so I tried to engage. "And what do you do, exactly?"

"I help them with English," she said, "for taking their GEDs. But I was thinking this week you and I could talk to them about adoption—"

I shrugged, the only response I could muster with no warning to this typically taboo topic between us. "Uh ... okay."

"Most of these girls aren't even considering it as an option. But I thought you and I could tell them our story."

Our story? What was that? "Okay."

Mom and I didn't really talk about my adoption. It was just too uncomfortable. How were we supposed to put words to a story that between us was wordless? But now Mom, with new lungs, also had new words.

Adoption felt too private to discuss with strangers—or Mom. I promptly changed the subject. "And what day are we going to Shell Factory, again?"

We drove to Butterfly House the next day while Jeff and Dad stayed home with the girls. I wasn't sure about it at all, but donned my best I-do-this-kind-of-thing-all-the-time-face and went along with it.

We arrived in the classroom Mom used, and over the course of fifteen minutes, three or four pregnant teenagers trickled in. Mom chatted with them about how their week had been and kept asking them if they knew where the others were. "They're late," she said.

Someone said one of the girls wasn't feeling well. Still relatively fresh from my own pregnancy, I could relate to sickness and fatigue. But Mom could not. She was on a mission. I knew she was disappointed not to have a bigger audience — to hear her, as well as meet me. She frowned disapprovingly.

Embarrassed by Mom's shameless agenda and obvious frustration, I tried to balance the awkwardness by casually chatting with the girls who had shown up. We ended up talking all about pregnancy and babies. These girls didn't seem any different than me, really. *What did I possibly have to offer them?* I kept thinking. *What am I supposed to talk about, anyway? Why had I agreed to this?*

Finally, Mom decided she would have to begin without the others who usually attended. To an audience of four, she launched into the story she so loved to share.

Here we go again, I thought, "her" *Butterfly Heaven* story. If it hadn't been for me crying in the street over a butterfly, she never would have taken me to church to find someone to explain what happens after living critters die. My adoption happened for a reason. She never would have found God herself. I'd heard it so many times, I only took in the high points.

Until my cue.

"And now Sara's a brand-new mom herself!"

Instinctively I tried to smile, feeling something like a TV game show glamour girl, flashing my pearly whites as if the curtains had just parted and the host had shouted out, "And now *you*, too, could be the proud new co-owner of a brand-new Toyota Corolla ... er, adoptee!"

But I really wanted to scream. It all felt so false. So wrong.

Instead, I kept on smiling. I tried to play it cool, show them I was the same as they were.

"*You* have a two-year-old?" one girl asked.

"Two kids!" Mom beamed. "A three-year-old, too!"

"But ... wow, you're so old!" another girl said.

Okay, so I'm not as similar as I'd thought.

It wasn't merely because I was more than twice their age, either.

Unlike me, these girls weren't afraid of speaking their true feelings. By their bold, fearless voices, I saw these expectant mothers as butterflies. Me? Stuck as a chrysalis, awkwardly pretending to be some poster caterpillar for adoption, but instead representing Team Go-Ahead-With-it-Now-Don't-Wait-Until-You're-Well-Into-Your-Wrinkled-Up-Thirties.

I stumbled through sharing my perspective on adoption in two minutes or less. Since I didn't really know what to say — Mom and I hadn't discussed it in advance because even talking about it under the guise of presentation prep was too awkward — I mostly just fielded questions. The usual ones, centering around my birth mother: How old was she when I was born? Did she stay in touch with me? Did I ever think about finding her?

They rubbed their pregnant bellies. I rubbed mine, as if my post-pregnancy pudge was as round and full as it had been two years earlier.

We weren't alike in several ways. It was obvious now. But as a mom I could hear the questions they were really asking: Would they maintain a connection to their child? Would we reunite? Did I think about my birth mom?

I knew the answers these girls' hearts wanted to hear.

I knew the answers I was sure Mom's heart wanted.

But what were my answers? A pulsing in my heart told me they were there, trying to burst free after being cocooned up for so many years. Could I tell the truth? Could I share that I thought about my birth mom all the time? That I looked for the face that matched mine just about everywhere I went?

No, I could not.

I squeezed out the mechanical, practiced lines I could recite to these girls in my trance-like state—"No, I'm not really curious" and "I usually don't even remember that I'm adopted"—lines that weren't supporting Mom's mission. But they were lines I figured would make Mom's heart happy. Even if they left mine feeling bleak.

I got lost in thought on the drive home. *Why would one of these girls consider adoption if it meant never hearing from her child again? Never knowing where her child was? To have her child grow up flatlined, numb, inhuman? To share with a roomful of people that she never thinks of her?*

Mom glanced at me. "You really don't want to find your birth mom?"

"No. Not really." I looked out the window, confused by her casual air. Why was she so open about this now, after decades of drinking up my robotic lines?

She rounded the corner, looking to her left, watching for traffic, as she made the turn. "I know her name."

Butterflies danced in my stomach. I looked over at Mom, yearning for her to say more, but too scared to show it.

"I wasn't supposed to see it," she continued. "But it was on some paperwork they had me sign at the hospital."

"Oh?" I said.

Mom nodded. "I wrote it down. I have it written on a piece of paper in my room for you. I wanted to be sure that you could have it, just in case I died before I got the transplant."

I quickly changed the subject. Thinking about rummaging through her room after her death, searching for that piece of paper with a name on it, my birth mother's name, was too much. One mother would have to die for me to find the other? But how else would I ever know what was written on it? I couldn't possibly ask now.

Fifteen minutes later, once we'd gotten home, I could not calm the butterflies. Mom and I sat in the family room, watching my freshly napped kids stack cardboard boxes into a precariously leaning tower. Before it toppled, before the noise, I just had to ask.

"What was it, by the way?"

"What?" asked Mom.

Crash. Down came the cardboard boxes. Violet and Olive giggled with delight.

"Her name. My birth mother's name?"

Two minutes later, I pretended to go to the bathroom. Instead, I walked straight to the guest room to flip up my laptop.

I didn't trust my memory. Didn't trust that I'd have the courage to bring it up with Mom ever again.

I opened up Word. I typed my birth mother's name. Diana Jo. Then hit save.

Someday, I'd need this. Someday, my wings would unfold. Mom may have come out the other side of her transplant a changed person, but I'd stayed the same. Though someday, surely, I'd find a way to free the truth in my heart that longed to fly.

CHAPTER FIFTEEN

Left Behind

Can a mother forget the infant at her breast, walk away from the
baby she bore?
—Isaiah 49:15 (MSG)

"Who left you?" Rebeca whispered.

I swallowed a gasp, the pointed question taking away my breath.
My birth mother. Abandoned me. Didn't want me. I didn't dare bring
these words — suddenly resuscitated from the coma of my heart, soul,
and mind — into the realm of the spoken.

The woman Rebeca had been addressing didn't speak, either.
Tammy sat in a circle with the other nine women in the group, each
of us sitting cross-legged atop yoga pillows on the basement floor.
Eventually, though, Tammy started to cry about her abandonment
wound — different, situationally, from mine, but the emotions and
their echoes remained the same.

Rebeca had directed us not to touch or comfort anyone who
became upset. Rather, we were at this weekend retreat to "simply
bear witness to each other as we venture into vulnerable territory in
order to discover what it is to become truly human." Sitting on the
other side of the circle, I didn't have to fight compassion from physically exerting itself, but I noticed the woman next to Tammy had to
stuff her hands under her pillow.

Tensions were already high. We'd just "witnessed" Dawn storm
out of the house after Rebeca had suggested that Dawn had a part in
her ex-husband's suicide attempt — telling her, too, that she enjoyed

playing the role of victim. It had been uncomfortable, and frightening, as Dawn yelled back at Rebeca from the stairs. "You don't even know the half of it! You don't know how much I've been through!" She ignored Rebeca's pleas to rejoin the circle and, after ten uncomfortable minutes locked in the bathroom while the rest of us sat silent and unmoving, Dawn eventually sped out the front door and never came back.

Conflict wasn't an area of comfort for me, and Rebeca's assessment of Dawn seemed a bit unfair. A part of me wanted to run out the door, too, but I didn't dare risk the group's attention shifting my way. I didn't know Dawn very well, nor was I privy to the full story behind her break-up. But I had just wrapped up a twelve-week parenting course with her, and had to admit that a lot of group discussions about parenting often got diverted to talking about Dawn's ex-husband. Besides, Rebeca was a credentialed therapist—a professional. Wasn't she trained to spot these kinds of things and call them out? I'd never encountered a therapist quite so direct, but earlier that morning Rebeca had warned us that she wasn't a conventional therapist ... and this wasn't group therapy, either. That renegade approach had appealed to me. That is, once I realized the retreat wasn't the casual mothers' getaway I initially thought I'd signed up to attend.

Even though I hadn't known what I was getting into that weekend, I had been hugely flattered when the retreat organizer told me it was Rebeca's suggestion that I come to the women's retreat. Ever since attending Rebeca's first presentation on parenting a year earlier, I'd attended all of her presentations whenever she'd travel from Idaho to Seattle to speak. In that year, I'd gone to three more of Rebeca's talks and enrolled in a Neufeld intensive that Rebeca facilitated, where I'd first met Dawn and several of the other women attending the retreat.

I had great admiration for Rebeca, and almost couldn't get enough of her advice and ideas for parenting. I tried to emulate her strong alpha-caring, feminine posture. But it didn't come naturally to me, not having been raised with these philosophies myself, so I posted reminders all over my house. "Collect before you direct," read a pink notecard taped to my bathroom mirror cabinet. "I'm the sun my kids need to be orbiting around," read another card, this one posted in my drinking glass cupboard. "<u>ALL</u> of you is invited to exist in my company," read the card above my computer monitor. So the thought of not only a weekend away from my mothering responsibilities, but also a chance to get closer to Rebeca—to absorb more of her immense wisdom, maybe even become her star pupil in that overachieving role so familiar to me—sounded ... well, divine.

When the emotional heat of the weekend spiked as Dawn left, what ultimately kept me from running out next was that hushed, "Who left you?"—not even directed at me. I'd be turning forty in less than a year. Time to open up my baggage—my abandonment wounds, my mother longing—set it all free.

I thought back to other experiences with therapists. The relationships were always so formal and forced, the way therapists refused to engage in small-talk, or stared with falsely "open" and blank stares, waiting for me to speak first and direct the session.

But I didn't need to be in charge. Wasn't that the problem? I'd been in charge of everything for practically all my life. I'd learned so much in the last year's deep dive into an attachment-based approach to parenting that it had become impossible to close my eyes to it— how my parents so often, unknowingly, put me in the driver's seat when I was young. While they probably thought their behavioral approach was simply "tough love" and all about consequences—in addition to hardening up my heart, their parenting style put me in charge of the shots. I had learned at an early age that how I behaved had a direct effect on how much love I got. I became a master at working for Mom's love and approval. Perform—through getting good grades, valuing the same things she did, pretending not to be shy, dating a lot of "cute boys," having a lot of friends, and becoming a cheerleader—and I could get all the love I wanted. I just couldn't let her down, lest the disapproving frowns that followed take that love away. After nearly forty years of intense perfectionism—now scattered to a neurotic drive to work for love, for approval everywhere and from everyone—I was literally drifting on fumes.

No, I needed someone else to be in charge for a change. I brushed off my concerns that had been raised when Rebeca mentioned that she lived "in community." It sounded off cult alarms in my mind when Rebeca spoke of her "teacher" and the women in her community who were "at source" for her. But the idea of having someone "at source" for me whenever I needed to call on her for support was starting to sound rather useful, enticing.

Later, after returning home and putting my toddlers to bed, I called Mom. Our recent trip to the Butterfly House and awkward adoption conversation still felt fresh, so I told Mom everything about the weekend retreat.

"So then she asked this woman, 'Who left you?'"

Mom gasped. The question took her breath away, too. "You're kidding. Did she ask you that, too? Did you tell her that you're adopted?"

"No," I said, recalling how I'd sat silent throughout most of the weekend, taking it all in rather wide-eyed. Through the three sessions of personal sharing, I'd vicariously studied the others and learned how similar we were to each other. Had this been coincidence? Or was some of my brokenness, my emotional scars, more normal than

I thought? A part of me had been relieved when we ran out of time before the retreat ended, before it was my turn for personal sharing. But a bigger part of me felt left behind, disappointed that I hadn't jumped in sooner.

I still wasn't used to talking to Mom about my adoption, though, so I didn't say more, except, "But I think I'll speak up next time."

CHAPTER SIXTEEN

Heart-First

The next best thing to being wise oneself is to live in a circle of those who are.
—C.S. Lewis

Two Buddhists, a closet Christian, an Atheist, a Unitarian, a Science of the Minder, and a handful of generally spiritual women walk out of a women's retreat together ...

No, not a joke. This was the place I found myself in when the weekend retreat formed into a women's group that met every two weeks with the goal of continuing to "share ourselves vulnerably" and "grow to our full potential."

After Mom found Jesus, she dove into Christianity heart-first by joining a neighborhood Bible study. She and eight other women met each week to discuss Christian books together, pray for each other, study the Bible, and talk about the pastor's Sunday sermon. Flash forward thirty-five years, and Mom's weekly Bible study had turned into lifelong friendships with women who laughed, cried, drank wine, played Bunco, volunteered at their kids' school, hosted gourmet dinner parties — and continued to study and pray together.

These women became a huge part of Mom's life — and by osmosis, also mine. In a traditional village, Mom's Bible study friends would have been considered aunties to me. Whether I called them that or not, Mom's closest gal pals essentially became extended family. I babysat for Suzanne's and Joyce's kids. Nancy's eldest daughter became my playmate and close friend. Marmee offered me safety from tornadoes. Amy and I moved into Andrea's house for a week while Mom and Dad sailed in Hawaii.

The friendship Mom shared with these strong, funny, caring, Biblical women got them through many of their life's trials, including a divorce, a child's unwed pregnancy, another child's suicide, and Mom's autoimmune disease. Their joys glued them together, too — sharing each other's kids' graduations, first jobs, and marriages — and later delighting in their forays into grandparenting.

I wanted to curate that kind of community for our family, too, and my women's group seemed like just the right opportunity. How nice it would be to finally release my abandonment-related baggage, and at the same time unearth a circle of support and love with the group of strong, confident, caring women I had gotten to know through Rebeca's retreat. The retreat had closed with one woman in crisis, so we all rallied around her by bringing her soup, calling to check in with her, or helping her out with childcare. A model like Mom's Bible Study ... not to mention, a caring, human way to serve others in need. The women's group was missing the Bible study and the shared faith. But most of the women seemed to have a sincere interest in spirituality and transformation. *What could be so wrong with that?*

I was the closet Christian. Or at least I thought I was ... but I had adopted my faith simply because it was handed to me by my parents and my upbringing in the Dutch Reformed, and then Lutheran, church. Maybe I stayed quiet about Christianity because I couldn't claim it as my own. *Or maybe this is what spirituality looks like for me,* I thought, with an odd mix of emotion that was just as uncomfortable, as giddy, deferring to Rebeca, who lived in a spiritual community that seemed to incorporate Hindu and Buddhist philosophies, as well as the psychologically spiritual work of Carl Jung. Rebeca even quoted Jesus at one point, which equally agitated me and put me at ease.

I grew incredibly close with the women in the group—fast. Through the Neufeld parenting model, we had learned that in attachment people first come together after being in proximity, then sharing things in common, and having a sense of belonging and loyalty. If all goes well, they grow to attach at deeper levels—feeling significant, falling in love, and, eventually, being known. The women's group bypassed these first important stages, skipping us straight to a level of being known—though on the surface, I had nothing in common with these women, other than the parenting approach that brought us to the first retreat.

"Where does Laura work?" Jeff asked when I came home from a women's group meeting one night.

"Um, I'm not sure," I said, though I could have told him all about her childhood insecurities, marital struggles, and manipulative mother.

"Does Kim live nearby?"

"I don't know."

"You've had a lot of meetings," Jeff noted with a furrowed brow. "How could you not have covered these basic things by now?"

I dismissed Jeff's concerns. He was in sales, after all, always thinking of great questions to ask, ever so adept at conversation. As I explained to him, the women's group bypassed small talk in favor of conversation about the big stuff. Our mothers. Our husbands. Our children. Sometimes, our resistance to coming to the women's group meetings. Whether we shared in common the smaller things, threads of our common humanity wove us together. Through the sharing I witnessed and the responses to my sharing, I almost felt … normal. Maybe I wasn't as broken as I'd thought. The women kept reassuring me of this, too.

As we entered a new year, Rebeca joined our group via Skype to tell us about another opportunity for a retreat: this one, an "essence restoration" seminar that a German woman named Uta, who was "at source" for Rebeca in her community, would be leading.

"I've done it several times," Rebeca told us. "It's like going through all of the different rooms in your house. Rage ... grief ..."

She mentioned a mattress. And a bucket, should anyone need to throw up. My mind, at that point, went foggy. *Um ... no thanks,* I thought, bewildered as I looked around the table and saw the other women smiling, nodding, accepting. *There's no way. Why would I need to go into those rooms? To the point of throwing up?*

Later that week, as I soaked in a sea of alarm, I set up a call with Rebeca and Uta to pepper them with questions. "You will be given nothing; no drugs, inhalants, hypnotism, nothing of that nature. This work is very grounded," Uta told me in her thick accent.

"Nothing will come up for you that you can't handle—it just doesn't work that way," Rebeca reassured me. "Both Uta and I will be there to hold you and provide you with what you need."

With remnants of fear quaking my fingers as I typed, I was the last in the group to respond as a "yes" to the seminar. I couldn't bear to be left behind again ... even though I vowed not to put the bucket to use.

To reassure the group, Rebeca emailed us:

I have been where some of you are sitting many, many times and what I have learned from being willing to stay in the fire is that there is no break-through without breakdown. The bigger the breakdown, the bigger the breakthrough. What some of you are experiencing right now is some degree of breakdown in response to the possibility that is before you, a possibility that is essentially a vehicle for breakthrough.

What is coming up for you has always been there inside; you are simply

being given an opportunity to see and experience it, which is the only way
you will ever have choice.

While the word "breakdown" didn't comfort me, I knew I had emotional baggage to attend to. It was time. Like Mom had done when she embraced her spiritual path, I knew I had to dive in heart-first. Besides, Mom always said I never did anything halfway.

CHAPTER SEVENTEEN

Camouflage Removal

Let the tears roll like a river, day and night, and keep at it—no time-outs. Keep those tears flowing!
—Lamentations 2:18 (MSG)

"I can't do this." I said. "I can't."

"Just try." Uta pointed at Rebeca, who sat in a chair facing me, just a few feet away. "This is your mom. Talk to her. Tell your mom what she needs to hear."

"I can't." I didn't want to pretend Rebeca was my mother while the rest of the women with me at the "essence restoration" seminar watched. "Just … just … Never mind. I'm not ready. Forget I said anything."

Rebeca shook her head while I tried to inch my chair out of the middle of the circle and rejoin the eleven women sitting on their floor cushions around me. "Oh, no you don't," she said. "You're staying put."

"You can do this, Sara," Uta urged. "If not, you're just going to keep having these same issues with the women in your life."

I nodded. It was true. The news I'd received the night before from a fellow participant of the seminar who happened to know Rebeca's age had shocked me—so much so that I hadn't been able to sleep. I felt shaky and so nervous it felt like a hurricane raged inside my stomach.

It turned out Rebeca was only six years older than me. I found this mortifying. What could it be, besides a testament to my complete immaturity? Worse, I'd been blinded by what I wanted to see, what I needed to believe, what I didn't even realize I'd been yearning for until I asked my new friend Christine the question: "How old do you think Rebeca is?"

I expected Christine to tell me Rebeca was fifteen years older than me. That would make her fifty-something. More and more, over the course of the last year, I'd been wondering if Rebeca was my wise, long-lost birth mother finally coming to seek me out, wanting to know me. *This is the way she feels most comfortable finding me. Anonymously, nonintrusively through leading this women's group, where I'd share parts of myself and she'd finally get to know her daughter.* Rebeca had been the one to suggest I attend that first retreat, after all.

But no. Not only was my birth mother not Madonna. She wasn't Rebeca. How many other women had there been? How many women had I been sure, at one point or another, must be my "real" mom, come to find me at last? How many fleeting fantasies had I entertained throughout my life?

I stayed up all night, flooded with awareness of all the birth mothers who'd come and gone through my imaginative life. Alan's mom. Another boyfriend's mom. Aunt Carol. Cool, smart, creative Kathy, the head of an advertising agency I used to work with. And the countless others who never even made a successful crossing from my unconscious to the conscious.

None of these women were my mother. They were just amazing women I happened to admire: mentors, not mothers.

Whoever my mother was, she wasn't here now. She wasn't coming to find me. The colorful display I thought I'd been putting on — trying to stand out for her, making sure she'd notice me when she came — slammed to a dark, abrupt, frightening end when I realized that all this time I'd been camouflaged, stationary — my wings folded up and blending in with my surroundings.

Uta pulled me back into the seminar room with her soft German accent. "Your mom will be able to feel your energy. She wants to hear."

"No. No," I sobbed. Then, I got confused. Wait … which mom was Uta talking about? Rebeca, who was sitting on a chair facing me, waiting for me to pretend she was my mother? My birth mother, whom I thought of as my "real" mother? Or my adoptive mom — also known as Mom?

It had only been a year-and-a-half since Mom received her lung transplant. She was still so fragile — unable to eat out at restaurants, her body too susceptible to bacteria. We had to wash lettuce three to five times just to make her a salad. Instead of hugging her when we flew in for visits, we'd run straight to the shower to scrub away germs. Sometimes we'd wear masks to be sure we hadn't caught a cold on the airplane that we might pass on to her.

But Mom had always seemed fragile. What about that time I made her cry after she discovered my post-shower photo? She'd cried the time I inquired about birth control, too. Then there were the times she shut herself in her room after I threatened to go and find my "real" mother.

But I'd be turning forty in less than six months. I'd be the same age as my former co-worker Gary, when he found his birth mother. My psychological midlife clock was ticking. My babies were turning into children. It was only so long before they realized their mother was damaged goods, before I reached the limits of what I could do for them. I couldn't let these fantasies, the unknown, keep haunting me, and yet …

"It'll kill her! I don't want to kill my mom," I cried to Uta. "I believe you that she'll feel it. And I know it will kill her!"

Ten minutes later, I'm lying on my back on a mattress on the side of the room after Uta had invited me to transition to the official "essence restoration" session. Once on the mattress—the symbolic tool to help people "look closer at themselves in an honest, friendly, and compassionate way and experience what it is to truly express oneself authentically"—Uta kneels over my head, while Rebeca and the rest of the women move closer to the mattress to form a half-circle around me there.

I'm crying. Crying like I haven't cried since my Alan heartbreaks from high school. I'm hardly hearing Uta prompting me with questions about how old I am, who's there, what I'm feeling.

Through my tears, everything blurs. A water line cuts off the lower half of my vision. A blur of green, what I know are the evergreen trees just outside the window, frame the upper half of my vision. I feel as if I could easily drown in all this sadness and grief. Never come back up for air, or life, again.

I'm wading through years and years of accumulated sadness. Most of it impossible to put into words. My life's losses in silent, sad images. So many of the images, and their tears, are centered around my birth mother.

I'm in a crib. Alone. Lonely. Crying. *Where is she?*

I'm in fifth grade, my fingers flying across the piano playing Frederic Chopin's *Fantasie-Impromptu* in front of the whole school. "I'm always chasing rainbows. Watching clouds drift on by ..."— Judy Garland's voice that accompanied the melody sang along in my head. *Was she there? Was she proud?*

I'm a gymnast, at a camp in Houston run by the world-renown coach Béla Károlyi. I'm fine-tuning my double-back tuck on the floor with a different coach when Bela takes notice. From across the room I hear, "Very good! Very good!" in his thick Romanian accent and realize, once I land, he's talking to me. It's a rush — to catch the attention of the coach of my heroes Nadia Comaneci and Mary Lou Retton. *Had I caught her attention, too?*

I'm a college cheerleader, getting launched in the air in a football stadium. Soaring up, up, up — fourteen feet into the sky in a basket toss. It took so much effort. I had an aversion to heights, actually. Drunk students chant and whoop. The band's tubas sound. Trumpets blare. I nail my straddle jump at just the right beat to the school fight song, just the right play on the football field. *Is she there? Is she watching? Mom is. But where is she? Notice me!*

I'm on a stage presenting at a conference filled with hundreds of people. *Would I be able to spot her in the crowds?* Applause. Accolades. Accepting a "Member of the Year" award in front of a thousand. But why only silence from *her*? *Why doesn't she want me? Why hasn't she come to find me yet?*

Uta asks me to try and talk.

"I'm tired," I say. "I'm just so tired. I've been working so hard for her to notice. Why doesn't she notice me? I can't do this anymore."

Tears for my birth mom roll into more tears. Other tears.

"Are you done?" Uta asks.

I'm hardly getting started. I hold up my hands to study them. They're cramped and feel buzzy. Hurting. My right hand looks like it's holding a pen, getting ready to write. But there is no pen. Ignoring my hand that's sending invisible words airborne, I surprise myself by yelling.

"I'm no better than my birth mom. No, I'm worse. I killed my baby."

I'm shocked by my rush of words. I hadn't been thinking about that day. Ever. I made a point of not thinking about that day.

I expect a bewildered or judgmental remark. I expect the session to come to a screeching halt. For Uta to shame me, give up on me. I anticipate confusion, questions — the answers to which I'll have to spell out.

Unfazed, though, Uta interrupts. "Can you see your baby?"

"No," I say. *Baby?*

"Is it a boy or a girl?" Uta asks.

There was no baby. I can't think about a baby. I'm a rescuer of butter-flies, prairie dogs, turtles, lonely infants. I can't afford to consider it a baby.

"A girl," I guess, hoping to move on.

"What would the baby be saying to you? See if you can hear what she is saying to you."

It was nothing. It was supposed to have been nothing. Discarded, cast away — like I had been. My birth mother hadn't looked back. Why should I?

I sob, though, realizing I can't not look back. It's not in my nature. "She says she's okay. She's with my sister's baby, Kenna, and she's okay."

"She forgives you," Uta says, both a question and a statement in her tone.

"Yes," I say.

Snapped back to the present, I'm aware of the other women attending the retreat. I hadn't forgotten they were there, but I'd been trying not to think about them. I don't cry in front of other people. I hardly cry alone. This had not been easy. I hadn't been thoughtful with what I was sharing, either, the way those words just flew without thought.

Two women from my women's group were raising adopted daughters. An older woman who'd gone before me had just shed tears for the son she gave up for adoption. Christine, also adopted, had suffered five miscarriages. How insensitive of me to be talking about all of this in front of these people. The last thing I intended was to hurt anyone.

I sit up, stunned to see everyone in the room crying.

I turn to Christine. "I'm sorry."

She asks if it's okay to come hug me and we sit on the mattress, embraced in each other's arms. Uta urges everyone to find a partner to hold, too.

I sit there hugging Christine for a minute or two, and then look over her shoulder through the window — lest I focus too much on the awkwardness of being locked in an embrace with a person I hardly know ... and already suffering from what Dr. Brené Brown kindly calls a "vulnerability hangover."[1]

The blurred evergreen trees outside come into focus again. I can see the detail of each and every pine needle. It reminds me of going skiing for the first time after my laser eye surgery. Neither glasses nor contacts had been able to capture sharpness like that. I'd never realized trees could be so pretty, made up of so many parts — branches, needles, buds, cones. Looking out the window, in awe of the crisp evergreens, it feels like my vision has just been corrected again, only instead of through surgery, tears.

I wasn't sure what had just happened, but my camouflage had been removed. I felt totally exposed and completely airy, both at once.

A Letter from Mom

By Linda Easterly, to Sara

Dear Sara,

I want to make sure I write this letter today—Sunday—before we know the results of cheerleading. I've never been as proud of you as I was yesterday. You did SO well, looked so pretty, and held up under more grueling pressure than I have ever experienced. Mostly, I want you to know that you've been covered by so much prayer about this that however it comes out is how it's supposed to. If you make it, there is an important reason why, and if you don't, it's because it would have been a mistake in your life.

I can't believe the strength you have (emotionally, I mean) to take on such big competition! You really are going to be able to handle any-thing that comes your way from building such strength. Don't ever think there is any problem too big for you—you're a tough cookie!

I worry about how much pressure you put on yourself. Please don't think you need to prove anything to me! I love you more than life itself no matter what you do or don't do. I see so much goodness in you, but I know you have a rough time when stress gets too high. I just want you to learn to enjoy yourself and the people in your world. Don't be critical of either.

Although I aged ten years yesterday, I'm so glad I came to watch you. I actually thanked God that He put someone in my life that I loved so much, my heart nearly bursts.

No matter how this thing comes out, I love you and I'm proud of you and I wouldn't change one thing about you!

Mom

CHAPTER EIGHTEEN

Meaning Everywhere

You're blessed when you care. At the moment of being "care-full," you find yourselves cared for. You're blessed when you get your inside world—your mind and heart—put right. Then you can see God in the outside world.
— Matthew 5:7-8 (MSG)

A few hours after I'd sobbed my heart out on a mattress in front of eleven women and the seminar leaders, I returned home. Caught in a tornado of swirling emotions leading up to the seminar, I had forgotten it was April Fool's, which had always been one of my favorite days. I delighted in pranking people—especially Mom, Dad, and Amy. Over the years they'd been getting harder and harder to fool, though I could tell they still secretly delighted in my attempts, even the failed ones. But this year April 1st hadn't even blipped on my radar. Did they wonder why I didn't call? Was Dad disappointed I didn't put an ad in the paper listing his car for sale for an insultingly low price, or that he didn't get an official letter from the phone company asking for back payment on twelve years of newly discovered unpaid bills? Had Mom been waiting for me to call at midnight, pretending I was in jail with a "duey" and asking her to bail me out?

My daughters were already asleep by the time I arrived back home, which gave me a solid chunk of time with Jeff to share the story of my weekend with him. He listened, in stunned silence, while I spoke—perhaps because I never paused for his vocal insertions … let alone to take a breath. Once, while dating Alan, I tripped on acid. The experience had been so alarming and seemingly endless that I ran into my parents' bedroom to wake up Mom, who stayed by my side all through the night to listen to my jabbering until the sun finally began to rise. Coming home from the seminar left my brain fired in the same way. I felt overflowing with insight to share with Jeff. As I recapped what had transpired while lying on the mattress, my hands got tingly again, just as they had at the seminar. My fingers cramped up as if I were holding a pen, ready to write it all down.

I apologized to Jeff. Not for the incessant jabbering. Frankly, he was used to me talking a lot. But as we spoke, I realized how I'd spent our relationship waiting for him to rescue me — all the ways I'd been expecting him to be "mommy" to me, to come save me, to make all my pain go away. All the ways that waiting led me to disappointment and frustration. Tears cascaded down his cheeks at the same time his face softened, a great burden visibly lifted.

Our powerful connection helped lull me to sleep ... at least for a few hours.

But I woke up at 4:00 a.m., overflowing with more insights, along with a keen awareness of my continued suffering. So much emotion had been released over the weekend, but I still had so much more to let out. I hadn't been kidding when I told Uta that I was only getting started. I wrote Rebeca a long and manic email, telling her about my night with Jeff, raving about how beautiful and strong and scary she'd been while leading the seminar, asking her what to do next with all of this grief I needed to attend to — and for her thoughts on finding my way back into relationship with Mom:

> i felt her feel me yesterday when i was calling for her. and she didn't come. and i also had this massive moment of realization that the day i had the abortion, i had called in sick to work, my first job, and that was a big big deal for me, being so scared i'd get caught in my lie. and then the second i got home to my apartment with my boyfriend, my mom called. in the middle of the day, when she should have thought i was at work and she never called me at work. she had known. somehow that day i was calling

for her and i needed her and she knew it and felt it. She called me but didn't have the balls to ask me if i was okay. she was scared and panicky and wondering why i called in sick to work. i heard all of that, and it scared me too. she knew i was lying. and i know now that she knew. i've been hiding that secret from her all these years but she totally totally knew. And she wasn't there for me.

Just like that night on LSD in high school, I needed Mom now. My soul had called out for her from the seminar while leaking its suffering all over a mattress. But this time her soul didn't respond to mine.

I finished my email just as the rest of my family awoke. Too soon, breakfast was over and Jeff left for work, leaving me alone with the kids in a jarring state of emotional exhaustion and emotional high, as I continued to get bombarded with new insights about my life. I was also immobilized, stuck in the in-between land of striving to be The Perfect Parent who desperately wanted to make up for my time away from my daughters, but also in need of recovery time without having to attend to the incessant needs of my children.

To make matters worse, my mind couldn't stop looking for metaphors. Everything seemed to hold deep and sacred meaning. The girls grabbed for the iPad. "It's tempting to push all the buttons," I said, reflecting on my weekend at the seminar and all of the buttons I had symbolically pushed. "But you've got to push the buttons. You've got to see what will happen, or you'll never know."

Violet and Olive smiled as if I finally understood them, unaware that I'd turned into a philosopher overnight and had been talking about something deeper than screen-time limits.

"Hey, I have an idea. Let's go to the zoo today!" I announced. We loaded up in the car, blasting Raffi's "Mama's Taking Us to the Zoo Tomorrow" as we headed down the block.

I pulled over three times during the two-mile journey. First, to check my phone and find out if Rebeca had written back. (She hadn't.) Then, to write down the latest reflections in my journal, which I'd brilliantly remembered to throw into the diaper bag. I didn't want to miss capturing any of the insights that kept speeding toward me in the wake of my mattress undoing.

While we waited for a stoplight to change, Violet, my three-year-old back-seat driver, asked me why I wasn't turning.

"It's not our turn," I explained. "We have to wait for the green light."

Once the light changed and I made the turn, I narrated, "Okay, it's my turn now. I'm going!"

After completing the turn, I pulled over to jot this interaction down. *Look at that. I've been waiting for my turn – all my life. Now it's my turn! I am indeed going!*

As we walked up the city sidewalk to the zoo, we passed a free newspaper bin. Violet stared at the cover story, then reached into the bin to grab a paper. Normally, I probably would have rushed her along or told her not to touch. Now, though, I was full of patience as my daughter looked up at me with a question in her eyes: *Can I have it?*

I smiled. "Go ahead, take it. It's okay."

I looked at the cover to see what captivated her attention. A picture of two Care Bears. Amy had loved collecting Care Bears when we were little! *Caring bears … like the women in my women's group!* One even had a cloud with raindrops – or were they tears? – on his furry belly. *The bear that helps people grieve. Wow.* I paused, leaning on the newspaper bin to write down these reflections, too.

After leaving the zoo, we stopped for burritos. The parking lot at our favorite Mexican dive was under construction.

"Mama, why are there two dump trucks?" Violet pondered.

"Sometimes there's just a lot of stuff to dump." I got lost in thought, thinking of all the emotional anguish I'd just dumped over the weekend. As we walked through the parking lot, a loud crashing noise interrupted my thoughts as another big load was discarded into the truck.

Violet jumped. I swooped her up, recalling how loud I'd been only twenty-four hours before during my tempest of tears. "It's okay," I told her. "It was just some loud stuff that needed dumping. Sometimes getting rid of stuff can be loud."

On the way home, our bellies full of rice and beans and corn tortillas, Olive peppered me with the same question I felt like she'd been asking me for weeks now. "Who's gonna sit there?"

At this point I'd usually ask her "Sit where?" And we'd get going on one of those nonsensical conversation loops that so often happens while dialoguing with small children.

"Sit where, honey?" I repeated, per usual. This time, though, I glanced back at her, too, in an effort to be extra present, even if it was the same, circular conversation.

Olive pointed at the middle seat in the car.

Could it be? I started to cry. Was that seat for my unborn child? Or was it for the child in me—the abandoned little girl waiting to be seen, needing to be mothered?

I sobbed. "Another little girl's sitting there." Both my unborn child and my infantile self—I really could imagine driving all four of these girls around in the back seat. *Yes, I can be Mother to each of them. There is plenty of room in the car.* Oddly, for the first time Olive seemed satiated by the conversation and let it go.

As the day went on, the emotional drain on seeing metaphors everywhere began to wear me down. I made bad decisions. I took our aggressive dog Peetey on a walk with the kids. I believed he no longer needed the muzzle he wore ever since biting Violet a year earlier. Thankfully, he didn't bite either of my daughters that day, but it was a careless decision.

All through the day, I berated myself for taking so many breaks from my kids. But if I missed jotting down an insight, I berated myself for that, too. And as the day wore on, I grew more frantic in checking my email, looking for a reply from Rebeca. Nothing. I hadn't heard from any of the other women in the group, either, whom I'd reached out to as the day progressed. I began to shake. Had I done something wrong yesterday? Had I offended them? Had I gone completely Cuckoo for Cocoa Puffs?

Into my journal, I ferociously scribbled my thoughts and feelings:

Get out of yourself! Get out of your mind! CARE about these girls in front of you! They need you to care! They are you, too! You need to care! They are God speaking to you, too. CARE! Stop checking your email to see if people love you. They do! You already know that. You felt it yesterday and it's OKAY to believe in it. This is big stuff, YES! But you don't have to get every bit out RIGHT NOW. It's not going away. You're not going to lose it. CARE. The girls, Jeff, Peetey, and Lucy. NEED YOU TO CARE. You have things to give. Not because you don't deserve it. But because you CARE.

I slammed my journal shut. I turned off my cell phone. I tried to care. I remembered: "Caring makes us human." I wanted to be human again. How long had it been since I truly cared?

But my forced caring got muddled with my perfectionism.

Taking the girls outside, I told them to run into the street. "Mama will protect you. Don't worry!"

They looked up at me with furrowed brows, expecting me to laugh and remind them not to go in the street, like I normally said. But I urged them along. "Really, just try it and you'll see you're safe."

Finally, they stepped off the curb and looked back at me for approval as they jogged beside it. I jumped out boldly in front of them and feigned blocking away all the imaginary cars that were about to hit them. "Don't worry," I said in my God complex. "Mama will always protect you!"

Thankfully our sleepy street had no traffic at that time of day. So my motherly prowess ended at that and we went back home.

I checked email again. Still, nothing from Rebeca or any of the women in the women's group. I tried calling Rebeca. Her phone was turned off, going straight to voicemail. *Why isn't she there? Why isn't anyone there? I need help.*

Where is she? Notice me!

Jeff walked in from work just as I'd coaxed one of the girls into freely urinating in the play room. "Don't worry—just let it all out!" I'd said.

Jeff looked at me as if a stranger. I was a stranger, in fact, to us all.

He called the girls out of the play room for a snack. Dinner hadn't even been considered and little bellies were hungry. But by this point, I'd reached the point of obsession. I shooed Jeff away so I could convince our daughter to freely poop. I never wanted my precious girl to end up like me, being washed over by a tsunami of repressed emotion someday. I had to make room for any stuckness … and decided it all began with her waste. *Surely this is why someone came up with the "Elimination Communication" potty-training method I'd remembered reading about.*

Rebeca called right then. I ran downstairs to take her call in private, leaving my stunned husband alone to clean up the mess and make dinner.

Rebeca didn't have time to talk, but she'd called my friend Christine, who was on her way over to my house.

Within minutes, Christine came over to pick me up and drive me back to Uta.

I was being rescued. Even though I ached to be rescued, the attempt was weak and didn't do much to quell the storm inside my heart.

CHAPTER NINETEEN

Kite Enlightenment

Wake up from your sleep, Climb out of your coffins; Christ will
show you the light!
—Ephesians 5:14 (MSG)

About a month after I'd attended the "essence restoration" seminar
and had finally returned to my "normal" self—thanks to heavy doses
of sleep, exercise, and time with supportive friends—my phone rang,
the caller ID showing me a 406 area code. A Montana number, I knew,
since so many people in my family lived there, too. *Including my birth
mother*—a quick thought, almost not registered, drifted into my mind.

"Hi, this is Sara," I answered.

"Sara Easterly?" The voice of an older woman asked. *Could be old
enough to be my mom—upper fifties, maybe? Sounded about right.*

"Yes." I consciously turned on my "work voice," which I hoped
sounded just as confident and together as usual.

"Oh! I found your website. I looked you up that way."

Could it be? As an author and publicist, naturally I had a website.
I'd also recently retired from running the local chapter of the Society
of Children's Writers and Illustrators, and still had my name scattered in many places in the children's book publishing world. *Finally,
one of these public channels led her to me!*

"I thought I'd call you," she said.

Uta had opened the seminar by sharing the story of a woman
who raged at her boyfriend privately on the mattress at a different
seminar. By the time the woman got home, her boyfriend had apolo-

gized. Somehow, he'd sensed the release of her emotional eruptions and it moved him to change. *Had my birth mom sensed me?*

"Okay?" I gave her the pregnant pause I'd been taught in journalism school, holding back my natural tendency to smooth over the awkward silence in hopes of keeping her talking.

"I'm an artist," she continued. "A public artist. I've designed kites that've been on exhibit all over Montana."

Yes. Of course, my mother is an artist. Where else would my artistic gifts come from?

"I've had installations in parks ... Last fall there was a festival down here ..."

I kept thinking about what Uta had said. *My birth mother must have known that I'd spent the seminar sobbing for her, asking why she hadn't come to find me, wondering when she finally would. Mom hadn't sensed my cries. Maybe my birth mother had.*

"You should see how beautiful these are ... So many people have been touched ... This last exhibit was huge, and took months and months to design ..."

But when would she get to the point? It almost seemed made up, all this talk and more talk about kites. I couldn't follow. Sure, there was a lot of chatter and wonder filling my head. But I was used to that. I still couldn't track the conversation.

She went on and on for twenty minutes about her kite installation projects. I politely listened. *Surely this is getting somewhere. Get to the point already!*

"Everyone tells me how amazing this project was, how beautiful these kites are. They represent beauty, life, love, youth ..."

I'd had enough. I no longer had the energy to usher in another birth mother candidate into my life, then wait and wait in hopes that she'd finally reveal herself. "Listen, this all sounds wonderful. But

I'm going to have to get off the phone now. What is it you're calling me for?"

"Well that's what I'm telling you. Children and kites ..."

I no longer cared if this woman was my birth mother. She sounded completely nuts.

"I'm sorry. But I don't understand. What can I help you with?"

"It would make such a wonderful children's book, don't you think?"

Oh. *That.*

I felt as if I'd been emotionally devoured.

Someone else wanting something from me. Wasn't that "the story of my life?" From the start, my life had been about someone — someone who couldn't get pregnant — wanting something from me. I'd spent my life working to be that child, and then the grandchild, employee, girlfriend, wife, mother, the long-lost child, someone else wanted.

The woman didn't notice I'd gone mute. On and on she talked.

"You should send out an announcement to all of your contacts ... It just has to be a children's book ... Think about all of the visual opportunities for this book!"

She talked and talked while my stunned, angry state eventually turned into tears, silently making their way down my cheek. *This isn't my birth mom. She is never going to come and find me.*

Worried I might lose my ever-confident work voice, I told her I had to go. "Why don't you email me more information and a summary of what you're looking for? I'll see what I can do."

"Write this down," she insisted. "This is my website address. You can go look it up."

"Can you just email it to me, please?"

She ignored me, pressing on. "Did you write it down? It's all there. You will find everything there. I'll give it to you again to be sure you got it right."

"Sure," I said, dutifully jotting down the URL in my notebook, despite my shaky hand.

I hung up, my hopes evaporated. These conversations, these letdowns, had happened hundreds of times before. Only this time I'd been paying attention. Awareness, actually feeling the rejection, may have stung worse.

But the woman's endless rambling about kites enlightened me. If I cared so deeply about knowing my birth mother, why didn't I just go and find her myself?

CHAPTER TWENTY

Wanted

He heals the heartbroken and bandages their wounds.
—Psalm 147:3 (MSG)

I hadn't talked to Mom as honestly and vulnerably about my adoption since that day when I'd ranted to her about my broken Mickey Mouse watch. But it was time to talk to her again. I hoped this time maturity would be on my side as I walked into the Asian-Fusion restaurant to join Mom and Amy for lunch.

Only once I sat down, I wasn't feeling so mature. "So, I called Dad earlier to let him know I want to find my birth mom. You know Dad, though. He didn't have very much to say."

Mom gasped as she put her hands to her chest, bringing my greatest fear to life: this desire had great power. Power to kill. If not me, her. *She might literally go into a transplant rejection right here.*

She stared at me blankly as if waiting for the punch line. But there was no punch line. I'd taken a ridiculously casual, airy tone, as if expecting her to start criticizing Dad with me, rather than talking about the elephant sitting in the booth with us at P.F. Chang's. I felt terrible for Amy, awkwardly squashed behind the pachyderm. But I needed my sister's steady presence.

Mom began to cry. "I don't understand. You've always said you weren't interested in finding her."

"Yeah, I know," I said.

She glared at me. "So you were lying?"

Lying? Well, it's … complicated.

Hadn't I already hurt her by sharing hints of my desire? Didn't she used to cry in her room when I threatened to go find my "real" mom? Hadn't I been responding to *her* desire all this time? Making myself into the *Good Adoptee* she wanted me to be? Grateful, content?

I'd always thought Mom needed me like that. It was all her fault, wasn't it? But new memories crashed over me, agreeing I was a liar.

Mom had brought up my adoption after our visit to Butterfly House. *I* was the one who couldn't talk about it.

In high school, after I'd threatened to find my "real" mother, Mom had written me a letter:

> *Someday you may feel a need to find your natural mother. I'd like to be available to help you. I'd need to make sure we proceed in such a manner that we won't hurt her in the process. She very lovingly chose for you to be raised by a family that could provide a fair break for you — and I don't want to take a chance on injuring her in any way.*
>
> *I'm secure that your loyalty will not suddenly switch. We have become such a team (thru the good and the bad) that NO ONE will ever disrupt our relationship.*

Her letter scared me. I appreciated her words, but didn't know what to do with the emotions it stirred up. What was so bad that I needed a fair break to escape it? Why would my loyalty switch? Would my birth mother try to take me away from my family? Being separated from my family wasn't what I wanted. I filed Mom's letter away, but stayed silent …

… Until college, when I wrote Mom a letter and mentioned my desire to find my birth mom. Only I might as well have used invisible ink. I'd changed course by the end of the letter, anyway:

> *However, the more that I have thought about it, the more I really don't*

*even feel that I was ever not a "real" part of our family, so there really is no
need for me to pretend that anyone out there could actually care about me
equally to the way you do. I am sorry for using this against you in the past,
when I've been mad at you and Dad for grounding me or taking away my
car, but I want you to know that I am so grateful for all of your parenting,
and mostly, that I love you!*

I never found the courage to bring the written word off the page into
an actual conversation.

Years later, I shared an essay with her about deciding I didn't
want to find my birth mother. Mom loved it and with my permission
proudly shared it with her sister, mom, and closest friends.

Success. Daughter delighting her mother. Attending to Mom's
rejection issues through the harnessing of mine. I was working for
the outcome, working to guarantee her love. But the cost was sharing
my true self, cementing the feeling that the real me was broken and
needed to stay hidden away.

Was I lying? Yes, I guess I was.

I hadn't spoken my truth, being too afraid of disappointing
Mom, of losing her. I said the things I thought she needed to hear. I'd
lied to myself, too, thinking I could make myself believe the things I
wrote and said.

I couldn't blame Mom for being confused now. I tried to explain,
but then the server delivered the lettuce wraps we'd ordered that
now nobody wanted to eat.

Mom criticized her mom, my grandma, for always bringing up
my adoption, for saying someday I'd want to know. She criticized
me for the callous way I brought it up, and for not giving her any
warning.

"This is a lot for me to think about," she added. "A lot for me.
It'll be easy for you."

She told the story of one of Aunt Carol's friends who had reunited with her birth mother, who was apparently "trailer park trash."

"It was awful," Mom said. "At least your birth mother was a good kid. Your birth parents were religious — one was a Catholic, one a Lutheran. Not a hooker or anything."

"Oh good." I paused for the server to refill our water glasses as my mind spun. *Religious was the opposite of "trailer park trash?" If my birth mom lived in a trailer park, it would definitely be awful? She could have been a hooker? What if she was religious now? What if she wasn't religious then?* After the server left the table, I realized no words could possibly retract her harsh judging ... or pull me out of my stunned state.

"At the end of the day, I want what's best for you. More for your birth mother, to know you turned out okay." Mom dabbed at her wet eyes a little more. "I mean, *I* know why you were brought into the world — to make us all Christians. But your birth mother doesn't know that."

I swallowed my pain, my reality. I hadn't wanted to believe it before. *Really, my only raison d'être was to bring my family to religion?* She'd given that message subtly before, but there was no masking it now.

"You were such a tricky kid to raise," Mom went on, circling back for another attack.

"There's a great book about the adoptee's perspective, Mom. The one I told you about ..." I started to explain about the adoptee's experience of a "primal wound" and defensive traits common among adoptees, thinking it might help her understand my "trickiness."

"No. It was *you.* You were so hard to raise — always so ... dramatic. Always so *sensitive*. I don't know if anyone else could have handled you."

She waved me off with her hand and then turned away as if looking at my dramatic, sensitive face for too long would burn her eyes.

The server came back, bringing our bill folio. Amy reached for it and dropped in her credit card. She smiled apologetically at each of us, then mumbled something about how treating us to lunch was the least she could do.

Mom turned to me again. "Anyway, I know women who give up their babies for adoption are so much more at peace than women who have abortions, who can never get over the guilt."

"Mmm." I realized, then, that looking at Mom was burning my eyes, too. *Why would she say that? How would she know about that?* I studied the napkin in my lap and then placed it on the table.

Then, coldly, barely making eye contact with me, Mom began to rattle off information:

"Well, start by calling your uncle. He was in the same practice as the O.B."

"She was a junior or senior in high school. A red head."

"She'd had a change of heart."

"What do you mean?" I tried to sound casual. Mom seemed so full of venom, I didn't know that I could engage in much more conversation. But I had to know.

"She'd had a change of heart," Mom repeated.

A change of heart?

"But her parents said they'd cut her off ..." her voice trailed as she began to cry again. "Her parents would have cut her off if she'd kept you."

Mom was still crying when we said our goodbyes outside the restaurant. She didn't hug me back when I moved in to hug her. I made the first move, instinctively knowing, after decades of practice, my daughterly role of taking care of her hadn't changed. And I was hurting her. Again … with the ultimate betrayal. Worse than a note about trying to get high. Or a steamy, post-shower photo. This was the betrayal she had feared for my entire life.

"I love you, Mom," I offered.

She nodded, unsure, the question mark practically levitating above her head. She said nothing. I forced a smile and walked away.

Amy and Mom went the opposite direction to go shopping. I headed across the parking lot to drive home. Normally, there would have been plumes of chatter floating in my head — soft, almost imperceptible — chatter reminding me how much Mom and Amy are alike, how different I am. But for the first time, I didn't hear any chatter. I didn't worry about being an outsider.

She'd had a change of heart.

She'd wanted to keep me.

My birth mom had wanted me.

I looked over the top of my car, watching all the activity in the lot. People coming and going from their cars, Nordstrom bags hooked on their arms. How could the world be carrying on so?

She wanted me.

Wanted.

An innocent, simple word. A word with weight. To someone with a criminal record, it might be equally weighted, like a ball and chain. To me, "wanted" was loaded with the same kind of weight as all the water from the Puget Sound rushing up over Seattle in a tsunami.

I'm turning forty in three months and discovering the meaning of the word for the very first time.

Wanted.

My entire life had been built around the belief that I was broken and unwanted. Being, feeling, knowing I was completely and totally unlovable. Then trying to prove that wrong. Trying to be noticed.

Trying to be good enough, big enough, perfect enough to prove my worth, to be wanted.

I drove home, my mind spinning. My lungs heaved for air as the sobs began exploding from my throat. "Oh my God. Oh my God. Oh my God."

A man in the truck in front of me glanced nervously in his rearview mirror just before turning right onto the freeway onramp. I didn't worry about what I looked like. But it snapped me back to the moment enough to veer off onto a quieter back road, knowing this emotional state and speeds of seventy miles per hour don't go well together.

This was new for me. In similarly reckless circumstances I wouldn't have bothered. *So what if I die? I hope I do!* I would have thought. My tears began to dry. My driving became more focused as I reflected on my suicidal tendencies, the apathy I'd felt about dying ever since high school.

But just like that, I realized, my death wish had been curbed.

I can't die now. I can't die now.

She wanted me.

I'm wanted.

CHAPTER TWENTY-ONE

Death of a Dream Mother

There are more tears shed over answered prayers than over
unanswered prayers.
—Saint Teresa of Avila

"Honey ... honey!" Jeff's frantic tapping on my shoulder made me
want to stay asleep.

"Not now," I muttered, pulling the covers up over my head.

"Sorry to wake you up. This is worth it. Wait and see!"

He flicked on the light and I squinted — less from the brightness
than from my husband's glow. Lit up like a six-year-old on Christmas
morning, he pulled me out of bed.

"I found another picture!" he said. "A better one. It's just ... just,
wait till you see. I'm not going to say anything. I don't want to ruin
it. But you're going to be glad I woke you up for this!"

I didn't say a word. I'd fallen asleep only minutes earlier, having
sunk myself into a dreadful, flat state after seeing my birth mother's
picture for the first time.

The adoption search agent we'd hired had called right around
dinner time. When he told me my birth mom's name over the phone,
he added, "I know for a fact that your mom really loved you and was
coerced by an agent."

How would he know if she loved me or not? He said he hadn't
talked to her. We had to use an agency to conduct the search, since
there weren't many records from my "grey-market adoption." That
meant that my birth mother's permission, prompting a conversation,

wasn't necessary. *Maybe the agent says that to every adoptee. Some kind of rejected-child consolation gesture.* But I was still getting used to the feeling of being wanted, so hearing that my birth mother might have loved me lightened me even more.

After putting our daughters to bed, Jeff and I sat together in my office, side by side with our laptops, sleuthing all over the Internet to find traces of her online.

The first picture I'd found was an awful Facebook profile — a bad, out-of-focus thumbnail poorly cropped and composed, showcasing the ranch behind her more than the top of her face. I could only make out her bangs and the top half of her glasses.

My issue wasn't about the artistic merits of her profile picture, though. Even though the side profile hid most of her features, I'd seen enough to make up my mind. There was no way this woman could be my mother. After a lifetime of waiting, wondering, and searching — scanning each and every room I ever entered in hopes of seeing my idealized myself in her and finally finding her — there was nothing left to do with the devastation but sleep.

Nevertheless, Jeff's enthusiasm, only minutes later, stirred me enough to follow him back downstairs to the office. One glance at the computer screen, though, and I almost screamed.

"This is even worse!" I wailed. "Are you serious? You woke me up for this?"

There was nothing wrong with the picture. It was a professional photo taken in front of one of those rolled-up paper backgrounds that photographers cart around for school portraits. Why posing in front of dark, stormy clouds — where presumably a lightning bolt could flash down onto bare, unguarded shoulders any second — was considered professional struck me as bizarre. But I'd posed in front of those same cloudy backgrounds myself in countless school pictures as a child.

There was nothing wrong with *her*, either.

But she was not who I'd been looking for all these years.

My mother was fifteen when I was born—or so I'd first been told. Believing that had created a lifetime of imagery and a person who was frozen in time as far as my mind was concerned. By nature of being a teenager—and, I surmised, a carefree, sexually liberated one—I'd always imagined a young, hip, beautiful, teenage-type. My fantasy mother was supposed to grow up just enough to come and rescue me, whisk me away to a life where troubles, rejection, and suffering would never touch me. She was supposed to look like a cool older sister, or maybe a friend. She was supposed to look anything but motherly.

This woman looked … well, like a mother. She seemed kind, nice enough—sweet, even. She sported wire-framed glasses and dressed in a beige blouse speckled with petite mauve roses. She wore dainty earrings and a gold chain necklace.

A Rockwell kind of mother. The kind of mother dreams are made of … just not mine.

Besides, I already had a mother like that.

"Aren't you excited?" Jeff asked. "She looks just like you!"

I saw no similarities. I stared at her picture, still in disbelief.

Disbelief didn't fully describe my thoughts, though. What was it? Insulted? Maybe she wasn't a hot, young thing. But I was … wasn't I? At least my husband should think so! It was hard enough thinking about leaving my thirties without being told I looked like someone pushing sixty.

"Look at her eyes!" he said.

"You mean the glasses?" I shook my head. "I had laser surgery half a lifetime ago."

"Look at her hair!" Jeff grinned, looking back and forth between me and the computer screen, where he'd enlarged her picture to full screen.

Her image was so enormous I had to look away. "I don't have red hair, and I don't wear my bangs like that."

"Her smile!" he said. "Look at her smile!"

I said nothing. My husband's eyes continued ping-ponging between the picture and me, desperate for me to return his grin. I refused to play his silly game.

"Fine. Maybe the dimples." I zipped my lips closed, careful not to reveal my actual dimples and further feed his fervor. "Maybe I have her dimples. That's it, though."

I trudged up the stairs to go to bed. With every step, my feet felt heavier, requiring concentrated effort to make it up to the next one. That's when it struck—not disbelief, not insult. Loss. Grief. Mourning. I felt so alone. An orphan, no more hope left inside me. My mother wasn't Madonna. She wasn't Rebeca. She wasn't any of the others. One by one, I'd ruled them all out.

And here I was, ruling out a motherly looking mother. My *actual* birth mother. Who else was left?

PART II

Honor Your Mother

Honor your father and mother so that you'll live a long time
in the land that God, your God, is giving you.
—Exodus 20:12 (MSG)

CHAPTER TWENTY-TWO

Bridge Crossing

For God gave us a spirit not of fear, but of power and love and self-control.
—2 Timothy 1:7 (ESV)

I sat in my parked car, alone in a tucked-away parking spot near Seattle's forested section of Carkeek Park. I read over my script one more time. Through the speakers, Avril Lavigne's voice serenaded me with the song that had given me a final dose of awareness, pushing me beyond skeptically studying an Internet search picture to placing an actual phone call.

For the last month, I'd been listening to "I'm With You" on repeat almost everywhere I went. But the song I'd found romantic in my twenties meant something entirely different now, near the end of my thirties while searching for my birth mother. *I had thought she'd be here by now.* The young girl inside of me had always been wondering when she would be coming to take me home.

My birth mom wasn't coming to find me. I'd shed tears and more tears as this realization kept raining on my heart. But I was ready to move past the tears, ready to find out who the motherly woman with the glasses and bangs was. No more passively waiting to be found. Avril emotionally belted out lyrics that reflected my heart's longing for my birth mother. *I was with her.* Hadn't I always been? It was time for me to cross the bridge. It was time for me to find her.

I turned off the music and tapped her work number from the search report into my phone. I sucked in one last deep breath, and watched as a finger — mine, I guess — pressed the "talk" button.

"Hello?"

It didn't sound like her. The voice didn't match the picture, didn't match my expectation. I almost hung up.

Instead, I shakily held up the script that I'd neatly written into my notebook, not trusting any of this, even my name, to chance. "Hi. My name is Sara Easterly, calling from Seattle."

Silence. Nobody there.

I didn't have to hang up. My cell phone did it for me. It never occurred to me that choosing such a remote section of the wooded park wasn't very signal-savvy. Panicked, I turned on the car and drove out of the lot, glancing back and forth from the road to my phone to check the signal strength. As soon as three bubbles filled, I pulled over and dialed again.

"Hello?" said the voice again, the voice that didn't sound like my mother.

"Hi. My name is Sara Easterly, calling from Seattle," I repeated. "I am working on my family tree, looking for a Diana Jo who was in Montana in the early 1970s."

I sound like a solicitor. Now it's her turn to hang up on me.

"Is this a good time for you to talk about a private family matter?" I added.

"Sure," the woman's voice answered. Aloof. Indifferent.

Wrong person? Had the search agency made a mistake?

I proceeded to tell the woman my birth date, the hospital I was born in, and then, the name I'd paid $3,415 to get because the last name Mom had written down all those years ago wasn't correct. I told her I believed that woman, Diana Jo, had placed me for adoption.

I paused, waiting. I thought about hanging up again. I waited for her to hang up on me. Once more I checked the signal on my phone.

"That was me," she said.

I waited, unsure what to say next. I only had one more line left in the script that the search angel had emailed me. What would I say then? It hadn't occurred to me to script an entire conversation. Besides, I had no presumptions about how my birth mother might respond. I only had the mental and emotional strength to move forward with one tiny step at a time.

"I don't want to upset your life, but—"

"No. You're not," she interrupted.

More silence, as she waited for me to continue. I didn't know what else to do but finish off the script, reading now the part I'd prewritten myself.

"I've spent my life wondering about you, and where I came from. And after almost forty years have finally mustered the courage to find you."

"I've often wondered about you," she said, "and I thought your records were closed."

I wasn't sure what to say to cover the silence that followed, but the pause made me feel like I was imposing. Maybe she wanted the records closed. Maybe she'd wanted to be left alone. "I'm sorry to call you at work about a personal matter."

"No. Thanks for calling me," she said. "I'm really happy."

She didn't sound happy. But then again ... I didn't, either.

Then we both laughed nervously, admitting that neither of us really knew what to say next. We agreed to talk later, and set a day and time. Before we hung up, though, she quickly asked where I grew up. She said she was relieved to learn I'd had a sister. Coming from a big family, she had always worried about that. She asked what my adoptive parents were like, how they felt about my searching.

I felt a torrent of guilt as I thought of Mom, still crying every day, sending me emails and poems in the middle of the night, haunted by what I was doing. I thought of Dad, who'd reluctantly sent me the court paperwork, along with a Post-It note where he'd ominously written, "If you're really sure you want to open this door ..."

Not to mention, ever since I told Mom about wanting to find my birth mother, our conversations had been strained, full of turmoil. Every conversation required listening to Mom's feelings, consoling her through her tears, apologizing for the callous way I'd brought up my desire to search for my birth mother. She'd complain, again and again, that I'd given her no warning that this was coming. She didn't seem interested in my feelings. She refused my offers to join adoption support groups together. She rolled her eyes when I suggested adoption books to read.

She got mad at me for referring to Diane with the word "mom" in it, even if the word "birth" preceded it. "*I'm* your mom," she kept reminding me.

"Yeah, but what you're not seeing is that you're Mom with a capital M, mom," I said. "Actually, you're my all-caps MOM ... but she is a mom to me, too."

"Hmmm," Mom said.

"This is all still a little uncomfortable for them," I told Diane, "but ... I think they understand."

Later that afternoon, I emailed Diane a couple pictures of Jeff, the girls, and me. Mom's heart was aching, but Diane's had already started mending. She wrote back:

Sara,
Thank You! Thank You! Thank You!

The emotions that I am feeling now just cannot be described. I have always had hope that someday I would hear from you, but at the same time a little afraid. Now that it has become a reality, I am at a total loss of words which is probably explaining the way I am feeling now. I am going to try and call you, but it might take me a day or so to absorb everything. I know right now I will dial and hang up a million times. So if you bear with me, I will call and I will be happy to share anything that you would like to know. The pictures were great, which is part of my anxiety, seeing you is like looking in a mirror at myself.

Your family are all so beautiful, you must feel so lucky.

We'll talk soon,
Diane

Like looking in a mirror at herself? Maybe I was more like her than I'd first deduced from her pictures online.

I couldn't fully delight in the news, though. Mom had stopped sleeping. The cocktails of anti-rejection drugs she had to take weren't helping her cope with her emotions, either. During one phone call, she read me a letter she'd written in the middle of the night:

This isn't just about you.
Nature versus Nurture. We shall see. You may be nothing like them.
I don't want to share you.
I don't want it to change things.
Even though this is your issue, I have a crack through the middle of my heart.
I've lost the will to live.

My fears that my search might kill my mother had been based on some reality, after all. Breaking one mom's heart to heal another mother's heart. Not to mention, healing mine. But I didn't want to choose between hearts. I didn't want it to be two against one. Couldn't all three hearts be honored?

But how?

A week later, Diane and I had another phone conversation. We talked for almost three hours. She told me about her husband, the other three children she'd had, her grandchildren. She talked about one of her sisters, who was dying of cancer. She spoke of her twin aunts, one of whom took her in after my adoption.

And then she shared my birth story.

She told me how the decision to put me up for adoption came to be. My birth father's dad, who was going through a rough divorce at the time, pressured them not to marry, as Diane had hoped they'd do. She told me how she'd decided, though, just after I was born, not to go through with the adoption.

"Was that when your parents said they'd cut you off?" I asked, remembering when Mom blurted that out at P.F. Chang's.

"Oh no. Definitely not," Diane said. "I still remember the look on my mom's face when she found out…"

As she described it, Diane's mom Shirley, my birth grandmother, had been delighted and relieved when Diane told her she wanted to keep me. Shirley had dashed out of the hospital on a diaper and onesie procurement mission. But shortly after she left, while Diane was alone in the hospital room, the obstetrician — who, as I'd recently found out, worked with my adoptive uncle to facilitate my adoption — rattled her with a shame-quake.

"I don't care about you," the O.B. said. "We're done taking care of you. But that baby isn't going anywhere until you come to your senses."

Diane didn't argue with his illogic. She believed the doctor when he told her she didn't know what she was doing, that it was too late, that she was selfish.

Then my birth grandmother, Shirley, came back to the hospital, armed with diapers and other supplies, ready to take her daughter and first granddaughter home.

"It's not going to work out," Diane said to her mom.

Neither of them brought up the day, or the decision, again. Until I had called nearly forty years later.

Shirley never knew the doctor had been so cruel to her daughter. She just assumed that my birth father's family had called Diane while she was away to insist that my adoption go forward. Shirley didn't ask questions. Besides, Diane had gone silent. Diane never found out that her mom had been snapped at by the doctor, too—nor how Shirley had carried the diapers in her purse for the next two weeks, hoping something might change.

"I was pretty bashful, pretty shy," Diane said, crying. "I hope you don't hate me for not having the courage to follow my thoughts."

"No." I reached for a tissue. "I understand."

"Hopefully I'm not a disappointment to you," Diane said again.

"Of course not." I knew about not having the gumption to speak my voice. I knew the price that came with stifling the stirrings of my heart.

I thought about Mom, then—my adoptive mother—who knew these things, too.

All these years, four different women had been standing on a bridge—Mom, Diane, Shirley, and me. All of us stuck there, paying a price in some way.

One of us finally dared to venture across. Now the others had to cross, too.

CHAPTER TWENTY-THREE

Mom Lottery

In him we have obtained an inheritance, having been predestined
according to the purpose of him who works all things according
to the counsel of his will …
—Ephesians 1:11 (ESV)

After I'd spoken with Diane, I called Mom. I told her how my birth
mother had been shamed by the obstetrician—whom I'd Googled
to discover had died on the eve of my thirtieth birthday. This had
seemed slightly ironic—and, I couldn't help it, somehow satisfying.
*The doctor who had played with my fate died just before one of my milestone
birthdays. His fate forever linked to mine.*

"Interesting," Mom said. She told me then, for the first time, how
she and Dad had come to the hospital to get me.

"Wait …" I interrupted. "I thought the doctor brought me to
Aunt Carol's house in the middle of the night?"

That's what I'd been told. I'd always relished that part of my
adoption story. It seemed scandalous, exotic, avant-garde—the kind
of story a writer could mine someday. My fantasies knew that detail
intimately—a tiny baby bundle lolling around on the passenger seat,
just two days new and driving to meet my parents in the dark of
night.

"No, it wasn't the doctor. It was the attorney," she said. "But first
we went to the hospital to get you. Only something had come up. We
couldn't bring you home right then."

Now that I'd heard both mothers tell their pieces of the story, I
was certain I could deduce what must have come up. That's when

my birth mother had changed her mind about the adoption. That's when she'd decided to keep me. That's when she had the change of heart—the change of heart, still so new to me, that continued rewriting the story of my heart.

Had Mom made a fuss in the hospital that day? Or had she simply turned a blind eye, not bothering to find out what had come up? Who does that—takes a baby from someone else—without pausing to find out more? *Someone thinking only of herself.*

About a year after we'd started dating, Jeff and I found "our baby's" picture online. He lived in Burnaby, British Columbia, also home to infamous "Burnaby Joe" Sakic, the great hockey player. Like Joe, he was tall, fit, and dark-haired, and such a stud that he had only initials for a name: P.D.

At the time, he lived in temporary housing known by some other initials: S.P.C.A. But we planned to change his residency. Once we'd seen the photo of this striking border collie/greyhound/black lab mix—his ears lifted up like helicopter rotors ready for lift-off, his eyes so soulfully staring into the camera, the endearing white patch of fur on his chest and front paws—my soon-to-be-husband Jeff and I fell in love. We were ready to start our family and we knew it began by adopting this precious canine fella.

It hadn't looked very promising, though. I'd called the shelter on Thursday afternoon. The S.P.C.A. didn't allow for adoptions until the weekend. I was told that one of the volunteers who had walked him earlier in the week got first dibs on Saturday's adoptions, and this man had already expressed interest in P.D. But it didn't seem fair that I lived in another country, without the chance to volunteer. I offered to drive up from Seattle the next day to walk him, but I'd missed Walking Wednesday.

We showed up first thing Saturday morning anyway, hopeful, waiting outside for the shelter doors to open. After a brief introduction, one of the trainers told us we could take P.D. on a walk to get to know him. She reminded us it was unlikely we'd be able to adopt him, as the volunteer had seemed really interested. But just in case he didn't show up, we were welcome to take P.D. around the block to see what he was like. P.D. yanked on the leash all the way around the block, figuring out right away what a smitten sucker I was. He was right. His intelligence captured in the website photo was real. I wanted a dog — this dog — so badly I didn't mind his pulling. Besides, I had excited energy to burn, too. Why not step it up to a brisk jaunt?

By the time we returned from our walk, P.D.'s volunteer dog walker, who we'd hoped wouldn't show, was in the lobby waiting for him. So was a family of three who'd also decided he was "The One." I couldn't help my cracking heart. I started to cry when a shelter employee took P.D.'s leash from my hands, already so attached to this darling dog I couldn't bear the thought of not bringing him home. I glanced at the volunteer dog walker from the corner of my eye. He seemed like a real jerk — for no good reason, really ... except for wanting the same dog as us! I didn't bother looking at the family. Also jerks.

Jeff put his arm around me and whispered, "Do you want to look at some of the other dogs, or should we go?"

But I couldn't go. Or let it go.

We waited to get the attention of the shelter staff, who huddled together, talking.

"This doesn't seem fair," I asserted.

Miraculously, or accurately reading the emotional heat in the lobby, the shelter manager decided to hold a lottery. We all wrote down our names. We dropped them into a dog bowl. One of the shelter workers drew a name.

I couldn't believe it ... the name she pulled was ours!

I squealed. Jeff and I embraced. I raised my arms in victory. I didn't think much about the other people in the lobby. Now I was the biggest jerk in the room, inconsiderate of the others' feelings as I did a happy dance around this prized dog. Shortly thereafter we all bounced out the door—past the deflated volunteer dog walker, past the family and their crying child—to begin our new lives together.

From the moment our name had been drawn, I knew Peetey (as Mom aptly renamed him) was meant to be with us. It felt rigged—by the shelter employees, perhaps? Fate? Or God. Over the years, Peetey turned out to be a challenging dog with aggression issues. Once in a while I wondered what would have happened to him if he'd gone home with one of those other owners. I speculated that he might have been put down, and so I became even more confident that his destiny to join our family was divinely orchestrated.

Not only was Peetey meant to be with me, but both our souls seemed to be beautifully and perfectly matched. Peetey had some bark and some bite. But underneath his tough exterior, I saw his insecurities, his sensitivity, his big heart. I'd won the mom lottery.

I thought about Mom. She and Dad had driven all the way up from Denver to Billings to adopt a baby, to start their family. Their hearts expected that baby, loved her already. Aunt Carol had told me how much excitement permeated the air as she and my uncle worked with Mom and Dad to get the crib put together, to buy baby formula. Mom must have been torn apart to sense that someone else was interested, that my birth mother wanted me, after all.

A shopaholic, Mom never took "no" for an answer. She could hold her ground and talk her way to any outcome she wanted—bartering for a deal on a silver bracelet in Mexico, returning a blouse that she'd kept well past the ninety-day return policy, negotiating extra upgrades on a car, or substantially bringing down the price of a house—agreeing to buy one once, without remembering to consult Dad. Even if she hadn't needed to put her assertive skills to use this time, Mom was incredibly lucky. Things usually worked out in her favor—from discovering a beautiful shirt buried deep in the TJ Maxx sale rack that just happened to be in her exact size and fit, to getting a precise and difficult match for a double lung transplant. When Mom wanted something, she wanted it with the whole of her heart. And she almost always got her way.

Had the doctor been embarrassed? Frazzled by the emotional heat in his office? The doctor was a colleague of my cardiologist uncle's. He and my uncle had brokered my adoption, after all. The doctor's loyalty was with his colleague, whose determined, now heart-broken sister-in-law had driven all this way to retrieve her baby.

And so the adoption was rigged. By the biased doctor. My determined, lucky mother. Fate. God.

To honor Mom, I could understand that she wasn't so different from me. Like me, she just wanted to win the mom lottery.

But still ... I was no homeless dog. Honoring Mom was one thing. Forgiving, quite another.

Special Person

By Linda Easterly, to Sara

We all belong with someone
A special person just for me.
Several folks can be that someone
That's often called a family.

God scattered us across the earth
Some to the east and some out west
But He wanted us to find our person
The special ones who love us best.

You may share genes with your special one
You may just share your heart
You'll love that someone from very deep
You'll never want to part.

You may not have my blood, dear girl
But my heart is yours to keep
You are my precious little daughter,
My thought as I go to sleep.

CHAPTER TWENTY-FOUR

Chasing Rainbows

I'm putting my rainbow in the clouds, a sign of the covenant
between me and the Earth.
—Genesis 9:13 (MSG)

After Diane had a chance to talk with her two sons and daughter —
my half-siblings — along with their spouses, she arranged a weekend
to fly out to Seattle so that we could at last meet in person.

"I feel so good to have started letting people know," she wrote
me. "I feel like there is a light at the end of the rainbow!"

I'm always chasing rainbows. Watching clouds drifting by ...

Frederic Chopin's *Fantasie-Impromptu,* and my fifth-grade mash-
up to Judy Garland's lyrics, sang in my head.

Like me, Diane had a fear of heights. She said that she usually
chose road trips over flights, so I felt honored she was willing to
overcome her fears in order to hop on a plane to visit me. I was also
excited to have gleaned this similarity between us. Acrophobia ...
genetic? Who knew?

I'd overcome my disappointment upon finding out my birth
mother didn't match the fantasy idea of her that I'd been clinging to
over the years. Now, though, I was worried whether *she'd* be the one
disappointed.

During our first conversation, Diane remarked upon the picture
I'd sent. "It was just like looking in a mirror," she reiterated. Then she
earnestly told me about all the redheads in the family. It took me a
few minutes, but eventually I realized she thought I had red hair, too.

Aside from a bad hair mistake in my twenties when I'd dyed my hair a most unnatural shade of red-orange, and for a few months when I'd had a purple streak in my hair while pregnant with Violet, I'd always been either blonde or light brunette. Diane was so excited about our matching red hair, and talked so quickly about it as she rattled off the names of each family redhead, that there wasn't a chance to straighten her out.

After our call, I studied the pictures I'd sent again. Oddly, now that I was looking for it, my hair did seem to have hints of red, especially when out in the sun. I opened up various albums, planning to choose a different, more accurate image to send her. Picture after picture, though — in each one my hair could have been interpreted as strawberry blonde. It didn't make sense to send her any of the other pictures. What I would see as blonde, she'd still probably see as red. Besides, I liked having something else in common with her.

As the date of her visit approached, Diane wrote, "I do have butterflies running rampant inside of me. Our meeting is finally a reality and I can't wait. I will see you on Saturday. I don't think we need to wear flowers to recognize each other, we'll just know."

Butterflies, too?

Mom was with Diane and me throughout our weekend in Seattle, after all. Not physically. "I'm not there yet," Mom had said, when considering whether she'd ever be able to meet Diane in person herself. She hoped to be ready one day, though, she'd said. She wanted to thank Diane and share with her our story. *Butterfly Heaven,* I figured. But in person with us or not, I couldn't stop thinking about Mom the whole time. The irony of it all … all these years being with Mom, consumed so often by wonderings of my birth mom. Now, finally with my birth mom and consumed with wonderings about Mom.

What was she doing right then? Was she okay? She must be worried sick.

I felt mean, ungrateful. A traitor. Heart-breaker.

Until I remembered how broken my heart had been … for forty numbed-out years.

At the end of our day together, I dropped Diane off at her sister's house—only miles from my own home. Diane watched to be sure I got safely back in my car.

"I love you!" Diane surprised me by yelling out as I opened the car door. "Call me when you get home to let me know you got home okay, all right? I make all my kids do that."

Mom did that, too—no matter how old I got—professed her love as I left, reminded me to call. I should have felt extra lucky—two moms, now, caring about me. But Mom had made it clear she didn't want to share me. *She* was my mom. I was cheating.

After just a few hours together, Diane had accepted me as one of her kids, started treating me like one of her kids—treating Violet and Olive as granddaughters, too. A part of me definitely felt elated. But I also spent the drive home fretting. *Was my relationship with Diane moving too fast?* I pondered the levels of attachment, knowing I wasn't ready to go any deeper just yet. I needed more time to sort this all out.

When I got home, an email from Mom welcomed me. "I thought about you all day long," she wrote. "I prayed your hopes would be met."

Had my hopes been met? I wasn't really sure. Was it because of my allegiance confusion? Was it because I needed to slow things down?

Or, perhaps, was it because I didn't know how to stop searching, chasing ever-elusive rainbows?

CHAPTER TWENTY-FIVE

Mother Whiners

Listen to your father who gave you life, and do not despise your
mother when she is old.
—Proverbs 23:22 (ESV)

I come from a long line of mother whiners. Growing up, I heard
a lot of family folklore about my great-grandmother, Grandma
McPherson. I'd never met her because she died before I was born.
Some said from arthritis. Others snickered and said, "No, bitterness."

Whether I'd known her cruelty first hand or not, I'd heard
enough about Grandma McPherson from Mom, and Mom's mom,
to form opinions. "A real battle axe," she'd been called. I didn't
know what a battle axe was, exactly, the first time I heard that, but
the image it conjured sufficiently horrified me … into relishing the
stories about just how mean she had been. Our family's very own
Cruella de Vil.

As a teenager, it didn't take long to build a habit of complaining
with my friends about our mothers. Even if we didn't mean all the
things we whined about, it became the thing to do. "Ugh, my mother
again!" — timed with just the right dose of eye-rolling and lip curling.

Mom seemed to understand this dynamic — sanction it, even.
Once, when I felt pressured into attending a party that I didn't want
to go to but feared the social consequences, Mom said, "Blame it
on me. Say your annoying mother won't let you." She knew, from
her own experience as a daughter, how annoying mothers could be
sometimes and didn't mind embracing the role.

Twenty years later, I traded high school friends for the women's group as my haven for mother-whining. After so much time off from bitching about my mother, going back to it again felt familiar, comforting, useful.

I'd continued struggling—in a big way—with Mom's jealous reactions to finding my birth mother. She still couldn't have a conversation without either crying about it, being mad at me, or asking me to reassure her of my love. Instead of taking me up on my suggestion that we join an adoption support group, she'd send me emails.

> *One thing I've found you're wrong about ... you said it's not about me. But I'm afraid to a secondary level, it is. I dedicated my whole life to my family, even choosing a career that could keep me close. Yes, I wanted to be an architect, but that would have compromised my availability to you and Amy so I gave it up. So, to some degree, this is about me, too. And, more importantly, you're MY KID and I'm not prepared to give up as much as a hair from your head. On an intellectual level, I'm your biggest supporter in the search. On an emotional level, I'm scared to death.*

I asked her again to read *The Primal Wound*. How I wanted her to understand me! How I yearned for her to turn to page 154 and get a reality check when she read:

> There is often a failure to realize that the adoptive parents' feelings pale in comparison to the painful feelings experienced by their child due to that early separation. If anyone should be grateful for adoption, it is the adoptive parents. If they are having problems with the idea of their child's searching, they need to look into their own issues of 'ownership' or possession of their children, their own insecurities, and their need to still be in control of their adult children's lives.[1]

Rebeca and the women in the group offered solidarity. "Your mother is such a narcissist," the women said. When I woke up to discover another of Mom's middle-of-the-night distraught emails, I'd forward them to Rebeca and the women. "It is outrageous the extent to which you must take care of your mother," Rebeca once wrote back. "Her narcissism and manipulation are over the top." I soaked up their sympathy and advice on how to respond, as if unable to navigate this mother-daughter relationship without the help of a support team.

I got so caught up in mother-whining—ever on the lookout for fresh material to share—that I missed Mom's attempts to apologize. I dismissed her feelings. Worse, I began to resent her. I could barely look at her, she seemed so mean and bitter and old. I couldn't un-see the diagnosis we'd given her of Narcissist.

My allegiance had flopped. Contrary to Mom's fears, though, my loyalty hadn't been lost to my birth mother. My allegiance had gone completely to Rebeca and the women's group, where everything became about making my mom wrong.

All of our moms were wrong. It took me a while to notice this thread that kept us sewn together: at least eight women, including Rebeca, commiserating over their narcissistic mothers, too. Week after week we met, bashing our mothers toward the lofty goal of "personal transformation."

Somewhere along the line, though, the mother-whining stopped helping. Talking about my narcissistic mother was making me just as narcissistic as she. I lost my focus on parenting my children. Then I grew paranoid, worried about all the problems my daughters were sure to have with me when they were my age. I pictured them sitting in a circle on a floor cushion whining about me, citing all my wrongs without giving me an opportunity to explain myself or say that I was sorry. I knew Mom had tried her best—but it wasn't good enough for me. Surely my daughters would feel that way, too.

I felt mad at Mom, all the time. "In experiments with both children and college students, it has been noted that being encouraged to vent anger, rather than control it, does not assuage the anger, but instead inflames it," according to Verrier.[2]

I was growing sick of mother-whining, but also still sick of my mother. In the mother-void, I looked for and chose more and more hierarchical roles with Rebeca. In addition to her leadership of the women's group, she gave me personal therapy, marital therapy, and parenting consultations in exchange for my freelance support of her parenting presentations and marriage seminars. She advised the board of a nonprofit organization that I'd started with a subgroup of women from the women's group. She wasn't my birth mother, but through all of these overlapping roles, Rebeca became like a mother to me. She nurtured me. She told me she loved me. "You are a priority in my life, I love you and am deeply committed to you," she wrote. I felt my heart electrify.

I couldn't recall Mom being nurturing—supportive, yes. Nurturing, no.

As I looked back in time, thunderstorms weren't the only time Mom let me down in this regard. As a young girl, stepping on down escalators at the mall intimidated me. Mom didn't have patience for my fears, though. She'd step on without me, never looking back until reaching the bottom, ignoring my wails from the top that could last for up to ten minutes before I'd give up and search for an elevator. When I finally found Mom, she laughed at my "absurd" reactions. In my adult years, when Mom visited to meet newborn Violet, she wouldn't hold doors open for me, oblivious as I tried to maneuver an awkward stroller I hadn't yet mastered.

Now, making such a fuss over my adoption reunion. Hijacking my search, making it all about her—just like she'd hijacked my butterfly story.

"I'm almost forty years old, Mom," I told her. "It's not like I'm looking for another Mommy."

But ... wasn't that exactly what I was doing?

Rebeca normalized my emotions and fears, modeled soft feelings and vulnerability, was ready to hear all of my secrets. She held me accountable with steady love, saw my sensitivity as a gift—not a character flaw or a mother's cross to bear—and was ready to be my go-to person for any problem I encountered.

She became the perfect mother I'd always wanted and needed. No more mother-whining. I'd found everything my heart had been longing for.

CHAPTER TWENTY-SIX

Drama Desire

Be wary of false preachers who smile a lot, dripping with practiced sincerity. Chances are they are out to rip you off some way or other. Don't be impressed with charisma; look for character.
—Matthew 7:15-16 (MSG)

They called me Sarah Bernhardt as a child. I was born into a too-young generation to know who that was, but when Dad told me she was a dramatic French movie star and tragedienne, I loved the sound of it.

Around the time I turned three, my grandmother had started keeping recipe cards. While she was a wonderful cook, these cards weren't for her Swedish meatballs or her infamous cinnamon rolls. Instead, she used them to write down funny things I said or did. On one of my favorite recipe cards, she'd written: "Sara, stretched out dramatically on the living room floor, 'Papa left me here all alone and I'm getting ready to cry.'"

My family had me pegged. I've always had a penchant for drama. Not only was I dramatic, but I was constantly looking, perhaps even hoping for it. In ninth grade, my childhood sweetheart tickled me too hard one time. I promptly wrote to Oprah, "Do you think this sounds like domestic abuse?" Oprah didn't respond with the advice I hoped for, but I did get a glossy 8x10 photograph of my hero that stayed pinned on my bulletin board for years. (Oprah was another candidate for my birth mother, until I realized pesky details like skin color and age made my fantasy too unrealistic.)

My countless hours logged watching Oprah after school indeed set my imagination afire, yearning for more drama. Domestic abuse was out, and there wasn't a lot of drama to be found elsewhere in my upper middle-class upbringing that was tinged happy-go-easy, in spite of the inner turmoil I felt over secretly wondering about my birth mother. But perhaps I had some sort of adoption-related drama. I was a bastard child of my aunt's or uncle's! I came from a foreign orphanage! I particularly loved shows about reunited long-lost twins. Maybe I had one of those, too!

So when I found out that my adoption wasn't exactly straight forward, there was a titillating aspect to it ... even after learning that doctors shaming unmarried young mothers into relinquishing their babies was not unheard of in the "Baby Scoop Era," and considered legal. The suspicion that something might be amiss hadn't left me, even as an adult. I enjoyed the drama, playing the role of victim. Nancy Newton Verrier has said:

> It is important to keep in mind that adoptees *are* victims of manipulation of the gravest kind: the severing of their tie to their birth-mother and their biological roots. The feeling of being a victim is not just a fantasy, but a reality. Being abandoned often leaves one with a permanent feeling of being at the mercy of others.[1]

The drama-loving part of me finally felt a teensy bit satisfied. I hadn't been making up my sense of powerlessness.

Without Rebeca and the women's group, not only would I have been unable to muster the courage to speak up about wanting to find my birth mother, I also would have been lost handling the actual drama that ensued. The women held me up—listening to my phone calls, coming over for moral support, offering room for me to drain my faucet of pent-up tears, reading long-winded emails as I poured my heart out. Not to mention, normalizing the emotions and experiences that had shackled me with shame for so many years.

"Are you kidding, me?" Rebeca said in response to my embarrassment over how needy I recently felt after so many years of fierce, hard-hearted independence. "I had to be rescued from the closet, once, I was in such breakdown."

I was equally fascinated and horrified by this information, told to me on multiple occasions to make me feel better about my own breakdown.

"Breakdown is the only way to break-through," Rebeca kept repeating.

I had Rebeca on a pedestal, though. I didn't want to hear about her breakdowns. But, I figured, if I ever ended up huddled in the recesses of a dark closet, at least Rebeca would come rescue me there. Besides, maybe being a drama queen was indeed normal.

As time went on with the women's group, it certainly seemed that way. Now that we'd all "grown up" by looking at our mothers "honestly," the group stopped being about supporting one another, and more about perfecting each other. There was a lot of drama in that. Often someone would share something deeply personal, then another woman would suggest that she was responsible for the situation. The others would agree, and the energy would shift. They'd be smiling like sheep feigning love and support. But wolf-like, they'd bluntly blame whichever woman happened to be in "the hot seat" for thirty to forty excruciating minutes. One time I took a necessary break from the group, only to return to find several others mad at me for triggering their abandonment issues, for being so detached and disloyal, and for my tendency to "go away."

Like the rest of us, the two people Rebeca had appointed as "space holders" when she couldn't join us in person had started emulating Rebeca's mannerisms. After meetings when Rebeca couldn't join the group in person, the space holders would report back to her with details about what had transpired and would receive guidance on how to proceed. "It is my experience that groups dedicated to transformation only ultimately work when they are rooted in a context of hierarchy," Rebeca had told us. But Rebeca's keeping tabs on everyone created more drama — inspiring a sibling-like relationship between the women, competing to be Rebeca's "good child." I wasn't a space holder, but started acting like one, dropping in little tattles about the other women in conversation, things I knew Rebeca would dislike, to try to endear myself to her.

I began growing skeptical when Rebeca, fresh off a silent retreat, came back to lead a retreat for our group, telling multiple women they were narcissistic — including me. Later, as if to comfort us, she let it drop that she'd just been called a narcissist at her silent retreat. Without being an expert on projection, I thought our shared diagnosis seemed rather convenient. Narcissism, in fact, had lost its weight. It was just a buzz word — or, more accurately, a manifestation of cult-like thinking.

In fact, more and more I suspected the women's group might be a cult. I wasn't the only one who wondered about that. We'd all joked about it. "As long as you're not asking us to get naked and jump into a pond of cauliflower," one of the women said once with a nervous, hesitant laugh — a question disguised as a joke. Thankfully, nobody asked us to jump into a pond of cauliflower, so I talked myself out of my mistrust. I blamed it on my eye for drama, or what Rebeca often called my "writer's mind."

But just in case, I only skimmed most of the assigned books, usually stolen and morphed from Eastern religions. For the first time since attending church with my parents, I started bringing my family to a Christ-centered church every couple of weeks. I used the time the women's group was supposed to be meditating to mentally go through my next day's to-do list. And I thought about skipping most of the women's group meetings.

I resisted ... and yet kept searching for reasons not to resist. I hovered over the flame, as if waiting for just that one nugget of information to finally scream at me that this was definitively a cult. Then I'd know to get out.

One time I joined Rebeca and Uta for a morning of meditation. I was told to sit behind Rebeca – the appropriate spot as if she were "my teacher." After the meditating, Rebeca and Uta started chanting all of the names of their community's past teachers over and over.

Oh, God, please say I'm not in this cult, I prayed, hoping to deflect the fact that I was sitting cross-legged on the floor listening to cult members chant and obviously worship false gods. *This is it. Now I know.* But afterwards, Rebeca and I went for a walk through my neighborhood together. A normal thing to do. Cult members don't exercise, do they? I erased the chanting from my memory.

Rebeca's humanity is what ultimately woke me up. I started becoming cognizant of the way Rebeca charismatically drew out information about other group members. Rebeca's charm and giftedness at reading emotional dynamics had a way of drawing in each of our secrets, which ultimately would be used against us later. As an expert on attachment, she knew that divulging secrets had great power, and Rebeca used this to her advantage – sometimes sharing just as much as we did, so that therapy sessions felt like an intimate, two-way relationship, or a falling-in-love process.

I grew tired of the constant triangulation – how Rebeca was always divulging others' private details that they'd shared in personal therapy or private conversations. She had a lot of therapy clients in my social circles, and I knew much more about them than felt comfortable. I knew the reverse was true—that they knew more about me than I would have wanted, too.

In a tempest of drama, it also turned out that Rebeca had been having an intimate relationship with one of the women in our group, Kelly. In response to an urgent string of voicemails and an emergency visit by Rebeca, I left my sister's birthday party early to meet up with Rebeca, where she confessed her relationship privately to me. Then, she facilitated a six-hour women's group retreat to talk about it, out of which we all determined the need for an emergency "intervention" with Kelly. The next morning, her secret finally exposed and conscience cleared, Rebeca flew back home to Idaho while the rest of us facilitated a breakup with Kelly on Rebeca's behalf. The drama continued to spiral, though, with members from Rebeca's community getting involved and offering to provide our group with emotional support while Rebeca recovered.

Upon learning of their relationship, I saw all of Rebeca's lies exposed. The time she suggested that if my adoption search got intense and I needed someone to hold me, I should call Kelly—not Christine, whom I had first said I felt more comfortable with because she was an adoptee, too.

The time Kelly gossiped about Rebeca's ashram, peppering me with questions to find out if I knew what it was all about. But I'd learned that Kelly and Rebeca had been in relationship with each other before Kelly had joined our women's group—and had taken direction on how to proceed together from Rebeca's ashram leader. Kelly had plenty of information about Rebeca's ashram without any tidbits I could offer.

The time Kelly just happened to text that she loved me ... a few days after a therapy session with Rebeca, where it had become clear I had a hard time accepting love. I had seen Kelly as a close, trusted friend. But now realized she was merely acting as Rebeca's mole.

It was also a slam in the face. I wasn't "the chosen one." The burn of rejection felt all too familiar after a lifetime of unconsciously feeling that wound as an adoptee. Especially from someone I had glorified as a mother surrogate. Besides, hadn't I always been told I was chosen? Wasn't I always trying to prove that out? *The Chosen Baby* story was a lie.

Then there was the therapeutic betrayal. Almost incapable of parenting my children after opening myself up so raw at her essence restoration seminar, I needed Rebeca there as my therapist to make sense of my emotional journey and support me back to sanity. But after Rebeca confessed to her relationship with Kelly, she admitted that she hadn't been available because she'd been spending her time with Kelly. I thought about how I'd put my children in danger that day. What an irresponsible therapist Rebeca had turned out to be—drawing out repressed feelings in such a dramatic way, only to selfishly disappear.

Speaking about encounter groups, and in reference to an adoptee who "died as a result of a heart attack apparently brought on by the rage he was prodded to feel toward his birth mother," Verrier has written, "it is unconscionable to manipulate someone into a feeling … There is a big difference between allowing and supporting someone in his feelings and forcing him to feel something that the therapist or group facilitator thinks he should feel."[2]

Once I emerged from my post-mattress breakdown and searched for a different therapist to guide me back to healing, Kelly had accompanied me to an appointment to help me assess one of the therapists Jeff had found. It suddenly seemed clear why Rebeca involved Kelly, and why Kelly had pointed me back to working with Rebeca, instead. Cults don't want their members accessing "the real world." I needed watching over. As Alexandra Stein writes in *Terror, Love, and Brainwashing: Attachment in Cults and Totalitarian Systems*, "The ideology portrays the leader (and the group as proxy) as the one true safe haven—the comforter, source of all goodness, the infallible one to whom the follower must turn."[3] Not to mention, with the full story, most ethical therapists would have recommended reporting Rebeca to her licensing board for discipline.

All of the drama had been interesting—and the women's group had helped me find the courage to search for my birth mother. But the drama had become too real, the constant alarm unsustainable.

Finally, I severed ties with Rebeca.

It was a relief to have my intuition validated by Dr. Neufeld later as I had more interaction with him. I discovered he hadn't known the extent of what Rebeca had been doing in Seattle as she formed and led multiple women's groups, nor all the ways she'd been capitalizing on parents who'd been interested in his parenting courses in order to find the women. To help clear up similar confusion for others in the various women's groups she'd started, Dr. Neufeld traveled to Seattle to give a presentation on why "encounter groups"—also known as "conflict groups"—don't spur maturity, stressing that his science-based approach to the unfolding of human potential did not seek to interfere with people's personal religious beliefs or spiritual paths ... nor compete with couple and family time and interaction.

It hadn't been easy to break away from the pull. I had been swept up in not only the drama, but in a vulnerability trend—not grasping that vulnerability is meant to stay close—shared with the closest of loved ones, not essential strangers who didn't truly have an investment in my long-term health. I'd also been at a crossroads in my life—smacked with colossal emotions (and a lot of sleep deprivation) as a brand-new mom of two babies under two, combined with years of repressed feelings about my adoption that motherhood brought to the surface. And I'd been caught by the desire to belong that we're all born with—especially luring for me as an adoptee always trying to figure out where I belonged.

My desire for drama had settled. Even if the women's group had inspired a misunderstood expression of my vulnerability, I'd practiced sharing my heart. Through Rebeca, I'd gotten a taste of what it was like to honor a surrogate mother. She was a mother figure who didn't deserve that honor. But maybe someday, I could try it with Mom.

CHAPTER TWENTY-SEVEN

Transplanting Trouble

For everything there is a season, and a time for every matter
under heaven: a time to be born, and a time to die; a time to
plant, and a time to pluck up what is planted ...
—Ecclesiastes 3:1-2 (ESV)

When I reflect on Mom's health in the years that followed her transplant, I see how easy it is to take life for granted, to assume that once successfully transplanted, everything will be just fine.

Several years ago, Jeff and I moved a few plants from our front yard into the back yard. We'd been forced to relandscape after water came pouring into our basement during the first rainy season in our home, and it required digging down to the foundation to fix the problem. Many of the plants had to go in the process, but I couldn't bear to have our four rhododendrons ripped out and turned to mulch.

I owed the rhodies the move, I figured—they're Washington's state flower, after all. But more poignantly, rhododendrons had inspired the budding of my green thumb after a neighbor taught me the important practice of deadheading each June—not just to make the plant look better, but also to reduce the prevalence of fungus. Deadheading became an almost meditative practice for me, something akin to plucking my eyebrows, only the tranquility and satisfaction lasted a lot longer ... and the process more forgiving of a novice's mistakes.

Not everyone loves rhododendrons. Some gardeners in the Pacific Northwest consider them dated, an old lady's shrub. After the hole in our foundation was fixed, the landscaper we'd hired to help with the new garden design wasn't keen on their aesthetic. But an elderly lady, the one who'd lived in our house before we moved in, had clearly cherished them. Rhododendrons are slow-growing and ours were rather large, having been meticulously looked after for many, many years. It seemed especially important to honor their loving first caretaker.

All four rhododendron shrubs struggled after the move. One died right away. Another's leaves faded. But three of the plants survived. They never returned to their full glory again. But each May, for the next few years, their flowers still bloomed — white, pastel pink, fuchsia.

Until one summer, when one of the rhodies began to fade. Its leaves shriveled inward and turned crispy, their color turned a muted, yellowish-lime. The branches became brittle. When I pinched off the half-hearted flowers, I didn't hear that gratifying crisp, snapping sound. The new flower buds, underneath, looked like bitter raisins.

What went wrong?

Reflecting back over the years, I realized I'd taken for granted their delicate nature as transplants. They'd made it, so I stopped watering as often. Two summers in a row I'd completely forgotten to fertilize. I hadn't done any pruning in a few years, nor amended the soil to avoid root rot. In short, I'd forgotten to provide them the conditions they needed to flourish.

I watched, and I wished. I worried, too, especially when that year's winter blew in with unusual cold and snow. More than seventy percent of its evergreen leaves dropped, exposing the rhodie's bone-like branches.

Yet a few leaves remained and I clung to hope. Was the rhododendron resilient enough to make it? Or were the harsh conditions of this world — and my often-neglected back yard — too much for the vulnerable shrub?

🦋

Shortly after she hit the two-year mark of her double lung transplant, Mom began to resemble my frail rhododendron. The transplant had bought valuable time. My babies had grown old enough to hold on to memories of Grammy. I had mustered the courage to tell Mom the truth about my desire to search for my birth mother. Our relationship had begun to heal after I'd sought to replace Mom with Rebeca. But like my transplanted rhodie, after a couple of blossoming years Mom started to wither, too.

She tripped over a duffle bag and broke her shoulder in three places. Then she cut off the tip off her finger by accident. While unrelated to her transplant — innocent accidents that could befall anyone — soon after these health trials pulmonologists discovered two different kinds of fungus taking up residence in Mom's new lungs. *Root rot?* I wondered.

The incredible number of drugs Mom had to choke down — new ones to fight the fungus, plus the forty-some others to keep tricking her body into accepting the transplant — brought side effects she called "icky things." She gained weight from the high doses of prednisone. Though she was usually an optimist, "Pollyanna-ing along," as she liked to say, she sometimes seemed depressed, emotionally flat.

Mom's wildly insecure reactions to my reunion with my birth mother had likely been exaggerated by her drug-saturated emotions, even though it was almost impossible to recognize her tender state in the midst of viewing her as an angry, narcissistic, childish, bitter person.

Then, Mom's autoimmune disease — perhaps bored with its

advance on her lungs — began to storm her esophagus. A year later, after she'd made it just past three years with her new lungs, doctors officially diagnosed Mom in stage three chronic rejection from her lung transplant. Her highest level of lung function had dropped by 77 percent. There was no hope of her lungs improving. While her pulmonologist, confident as God, considered another transplant, Mom's decline was so rapid, her blood type so rare, it was unlikely she'd live long enough to get another match, let alone survive the grueling surgery. Even if she did, it would also mean living out the rest of her life encased in a safety bubble, never traveling (or shopping) again. Meanwhile, her esophagus kept getting worse, and that body part couldn't be replaced. Soon, Mom would require a permanent feeding tube and then she'd never get to enjoy a meal again.

Her next step was to grow beyond her circumstances ... by accepting them. She turned to hospice care and kept her trust in God. "He will be right beside me through this journey," she wrote in her final CaringBridge journal. "He knows the timing and it will be perfect."

As it turned out, growing beyond circumstances wasn't only for my rhodies or Mom.

In his developmental psychology course relevant to transplanting children through adoption, foster care, or divorce, Dr. Neufeld said that in organ transplanting we have a big problem: the organ has to be recognized as belonging to the individual. "Is it ours?" the body wants to know. If the answer is "no," it's considered a foreign body and the brain goes into an immune system reaction, which can kill the patient. Dr. Neufeld says it is the same in transplanting children. If the new attachment is not perceived as one of "our people," coming in through the existing attachments — "Is it ours?" — we are meant to have difficulty and resistance.[1]

Growing up, Mom liked to retell the story of my first few days of life. Within a couple of days of adopting me, she and Dad brought me to Hardin, Montana, to visit my mom's parents for the first time. Apparently, I cried nonstop.

"You've spoiled her already," Papa told Mom with his usual straight-faced, dry wit.

To an insecure twenty-four year-old mother, though, full of doubts notorious of most first-time mothers — let alone an adoptive mother who hadn't been gifted the luxury of nine months to emotionally prepare for her infant's arrival — all humor was lost. Mom began to cry on the spot, believing her dear old dad was right. It must be true. She had no idea what she was doing.

In actuality, I was more than likely inconsolable in the face of what Nancy Newton Verrier calls "the primal wound," reeling at the grief and loss of both my mother and my self. "No matter how much the mother wanted to keep her baby and no matter what the altruistic or intellectual reasons she had for relinquishing him or her," explains Verrier, *the child experiences the separation as abandonment.*"[2]

I think Mom enjoyed sharing this story so much because she'd conquered those new-mother doubts. Once she found her confidence as a mother, she could name the worries, laugh at them.

But what about the doubts she never named? Would I have been better off with my birth mother? Maybe Mom wasn't who I needed. Maybe she wasn't good enough for me. Maybe I wanted another mother more.

Because she never named them, or laughed them off, these worries went underground. They got tangled in the roots of our relationship, and stayed there, unseen, with a weed-like grip. Rather than tend the soil, it was easier for Mom to forget about my transplant. "I barely even remember you're adopted," she'd said, proudly, on many occasions. But as Dr. Neufeld explains, a divide is created and exasperated if the transplanted child cannot experience closeness with both attachments simultaneously. The answer to that question, "Is it ours?" if unanswered, must be no. And in comes the dark energy of attachment, which can include, among other things, resisting contact, seeing the other as annoying and irritating, and keeping secrets from — to name a few.[3]

In his studies of children who had experienced the loss of a parent through death, renowned British psychologist and attachment theorist John Bowlby articulated the important defensive process in the child as a part of mourning — defending against vulnerability and further loss.[4] Verrier wrote, "The fact that the child does not consciously remember the substitution of mothers does not diminish the impact of that experience. In fact the inability to consciously remember the experience may make the impact even more devastating and perplexing."[5]

If only Mom had had access to the body of work of these attachment experts when I was a child. Perhaps she wouldn't have taken my grief as a newborn so personally. Maybe her natural doubts would have been pruned at the bud. Maybe she would have had the confidence to honor my first caretaker by talking about her as I grew up, to help neutralize the competing attachment with my birth mother.

I wished I had discovered their psychological wisdom sooner, too. Maybe I wouldn't have been so frightened of further loss, more willing to risk sharing my real self. Maybe all of my energy for closeness and proximity wouldn't have gone to my fantasy birth mother, but to Mom — who instead got my resistance, my secret-keeping, my defensive and detached heart protecting me from further pain and loss. Maybe I would have been more forgiving of a novice's mistakes. Maybe my roots would have gone deeper. Deeper into loving my mom.

But by the time these maybes came to me and I became aware that I'd spent so much of my life in rejection from my adoptive mother, her lung transplant rejection was closing in on her life.

Besides, cognitive awareness is one thing. Matters of the heart? Well ... another.

Health Update

By Linda Easterly

Ok, girls. It's update time.
To let you know I'm doin fine.
My lungs are bein difficult!
I'm still waitin for that test result!

This old body is starting to be tricky
the meds make me feel oh-so icky.
Oh, I could just complain all day
I think I will, I'll start today.

My finger has a mind of its own
It points the way to the unknown.
My ears don't hardly work no more
I can hardly hear. That's for shore.

My teeth is startin to disappear
They'll all be gone soon I often fear.
The hair gets thinner every day
And I've given up on Oil of Olay.

I saw my forehead and then I knowed
That forty wild eyebrows did explode.
What the heck is that under the chin?
I musta swallowed a big pumpkin!

Where's all the energy I was known for?
Maybe it's resting up at the Broadmoor.
I could teach and cook and vacuum the house
And even still care for my spouse, the louse!

Now the serious stuff. Let's make it plain
I really do miss my brain.
It got me through many a test
But now it seems to want a rest.

Oh, oh I just found a good part!
I still have a healthy and happy heart
God lives in there so that makes it pure.
Okay. Now I'm happy again, FOR SURE!

CHAPTER TWENTY-EIGHT

Prodigal Daughter

We've been surrounded and battered by troubles, but we're not demoralized …
—2 Corinthians 4:8 (MSG)

I found myself back in Denver—finally accepting that Mom was dying, beginning to make sense of our complicated mother-daughter relationship, and daring, even, to envision something greater than assisting in a smooth death and planning a marvelous funeral.

The last eight months had given us some respite from the intense emotion that arose during the search for my birth mother. We still didn't talk about adoption or Diane much. Mom asked from time to time, but I censored myself, fretting that too much talk about my birth mom might set Mom off. Though she'd never apologized for the things she'd said and the way she'd behaved, Mom had at one point written, "Believe me, I'll come around to not feeling threatened by this. Might take me a while. I'm basically an insecure person." Though I'd found a new sense of inner peace, it was hard to undo a forty-year instinctual drive to take care of Mom's feelings.

I did talk openly with her, though, about Rebeca and the women's group. Mom had taken it well, actually. I expected her to be fearful, focused on the cult part of the story. Instead, she mostly expressed relief to find out it wasn't my birth mother who'd been stealing me away from her … especially since I had finally woken up and walked away from the women's group. It was a relief to me, too, not keeping the secret from Mom.

We'd made progress. But when I arrived back at her house that evening, all progress seemed to have evaporated.

"What's *she* doing here?" Mom asked Amy, scowling and gesturing her head in my direction as if I couldn't hear.

I felt like a child again, filled with fear over something I must have done wrong. Was I in trouble for having flown back to Seattle earlier that morning, for leaving her?

Amy smiled as she brightly reminded Mom, "Yeah, Sara came back to be with you, Mom! Isn't that great?"

Mom shrugged, her face full of contempt. She seemed bitter toward me, I could tell, but I didn't understand why. The emotional distance created by what I perceived as a shunning stirred up old anxiety in my heart.

The good daughter, bad daughter game Mom and I unconsciously played throughout my youth was making a comeback. Amy: the "good" one. Me: the "bad" one. Her prodigal daughter—no literal squanderer, but the one who was different. The adoptee, but also the daughter not a cookie-cutter version of her mother. The outsider, in so many ways.

Amy, with a mix of finesse and obliviousness, changed the subject and before long Mom was sleeping again, dying a little more.

I knew I wasn't really a bad daughter and had mostly stopped trying to become that person or disprove she existed. So I made a conscious effort to let it go ... until the next day when Mom needed help getting to the bathroom.

Getting her up from the bed required a significant physical feat since her breath and strength had weakened so much, and for dignity's sake Mom refused a catheter. Almost thirty minutes after our journey from the bed to the bathroom had begun, Amy and I finally got her there. But once we'd positioned her atop the porcelain throne—technically, a steel medical commode on loan from Hospice—Mom looked at me as if shocked by my presence. First, she glared at me. Then she turned away and told Amy, in a loud whisper full of disdain, that she didn't want me there.

Mom had never before been so blunt in her rejection. Still, the prick of her disapproving frown and what I perceived as her preference for my sister—her only biological daughter—felt all too familiar.

My worst nightmare seemed to be coming true. Mom couldn't die this way. Our "us" couldn't end this way—with Mom shunning me.

From a developmental perspective, "the most stressful experiences for a child are separation from those attached to, feelings of shame that are intense or prolonged, or being scared too much or for too long."[1] The emotional separation and shame Mom inadvertently poured into me in order to squeeze out her approved model of a daughter became a recipe for attachment anxiety. Combined with my sensitivity—both genetically determined by my redheaded birth mother (redheads are known to be more predisposed to sensitivity), and largely calibrated by prenatal and birth experiences—this threw me into a defense against vulnerability and lifetime struggle working to measure up, be perfect, feel important, and be loved … simultaneously for two mothers. I also became highly attuned to separation, and feeling rejected was very often my first read on situations. And really, how could I not go there in this moment, as Mom so pointedly expressed she didn't want me in her presence?

Only thanks to walking my own parenting journey and learning about attachment dynamics, I had more consciousness around my reactions. Searching for my birth mother and finding out that I had been wanted had reframed my sense of self. Instead of acting unconsciously out of fear, I could push aside the "I'm not wanted" or "I'm not good enough" narratives to make room for other internal dialogue to calm my separation-based anxieties. I'd also learned that "trauma creates a bias toward negative thinking."[2] As per the advice of Nancy Newton Verrier, "If you find yourself always interpreting things in a negative manner, then it is time to check out your assumptions."[3] Perhaps Mom was simply expressing a preference for Amy because she was a nurse. Everyone in the family knew what a wuss I was around blood and even a hint of grossness. Maybe it was Mom's way of protecting me from sensitive toilet matters. I knew, intuitively, that the dying can be rather childlike at times. Just as I knew better than to take my kids' bluntness personally, I made an effort not to give undue weight to Mom's dying words.

My heart hurt, sure. But attending to Mom was my priority — and this time, not so that she would see me as "good," or so I could mold myself into the perfect daughter, but rather because I genuinely wanted to be there for her. She wasn't a perfect mother, by any means. In so many ways, even before now, she'd rejected me — a child already brimming with rejection, prone to looking for it in every situation. But she was my mother. In spite of the rejection, she'd been there for me, too. I wanted to be there for her now.

This wasn't the time to lick my wounds. This was the time to rise above and be there for Mom ... whether she disapproved of her prodigal daughter or not.

CHAPTER TWENTY-NINE

The Vulnerable Path to Forgiveness

Be kind to one another, tenderhearted, forgiving one another, as God in Christ forgave you.
—Ephesians 4:32 (ESV)

Mom continued living in limbo, caught between two worlds. Sometimes she'd be with Amy, Dad, and me in her bedroom. Sometimes her eyes wouldn't be focusing on us, and we could see she was in the world where she was headed, which we could only presume to be heaven. The realness of this place and her access to it fascinated me. It was right there, right before Mom's eyes, and thus also right before mine. I couldn't be so close to it and have even a smidgeon of doubt about whether it was real, holy.

But it wasn't all rainbows and unicorns.

"I need to get back," Mom said.

"Get back where?" I asked.

"Where do you need to go?" Amy asked.

Mom, talking to us, and yet not talking to us, didn't answer our questions. "I didn't lie. Why are they lying?"

"Who's saying you lied?" I asked. "Who's 'they'?"

Maybe it was that drama-desire in me, but I couldn't help wondering if this was about my adoption. *Was Mom being punished over the shady circumstances?* I hated believing in a scary Judgment Day and vengeful image of an Old Testament God—the God I'd grown up fearing. And yet, I couldn't help thinking, lies are lies. There was a lifetime of lies there—my lifetime so far, at least. I hadn't confronted

Mom about the lies in the midst of the revelations around my adoption because, whether I admitted it or not, I'd known she was dying. Why pin her to the wall over details, too late to change now, when her days were so plainly numbered?

But if it's true we're all accountable for our actions someday, then Mom did have some answering to do. She'd lied about my birth mom's age. She'd lied to me, telling me she always openly talked about my adoption. She acted like her shocked, angry, hurt reactions were my fault for concealing my interest in finding my birth mother—when in fact I had expressed my desires on several occasions—she just hadn't wanted to let them in. She'd suggested my birth mom was lying about getting shamed by the doctor into proceeding with the adoption. She'd lied about my birth grandmother not being willing to help her raise me. And she'd played God with my life. She took it all for herself, made it her own. Worse, she never saw me. To do so would have hurt her too much. She should be accountable for all that, shouldn't she? As much as I'd wanted to drop it, I did still begrudge her.

"Forgiveness is one of the biggest issues between a mother and daughter," according to Blythe Daniel, co-author of *Mended: Restoring the Hearts of Mothers and Daughters*.[1] But was forgiving even in my genes? Studying the concept through my daughter, I wasn't so sure.

🦋

"I need to talk to you about Olive," Teacher Janice had said as soon as I'd arrived for preschool pick-up.

"Oh?" I asked, immediately alarmed. The teacher had made an exception to let my twenty-two-month-old daughter attend the cooperative preschool class. The class hadn't been full, and the preschool needed an extra body. Since big sister Violet was enrolled, and Olive was already potty-trained, Teacher Janice made an exception to let

Olive attend the preschool one year early. It was the first time I'd left Olive with the teacher and other parents. I'd been gone for no more than an hour — half the class time. *Did she have intense separation anxiety while I was away? Did one of those giant, rough-and-tumble three-year-olds pick on her?*

"I feel just terrible," Janice said. "One of the mothers smelled a poopy diaper and we assumed it was coming from Olive. So we took her to the bathroom to change her diaper."

"Oh." I laughed with relief. *Just one of those kinds of accidents.* I glanced over at Olive's cubby, looking for the Ziploc that held her spare clothes. "But Olive doesn't wear diapers anymore. I didn't even think to put her in a pull-up. Did you need to use her extra clothes?"

"Well it turned out it wasn't Olive who was stinky," Teacher Janice said. "But I think she was a little upset with me for checking."

"A little upset" turned out to be an understatement. Olive refused to talk to Teacher Janice for the next two years while she attended the preschool. Janice lives in our community and attends our church, and so we have constant reminders about Teacher Janice to inspire Olive's now infamous lore of diaper malfeasance.

"I hate Teacher Janice!" Olive exclaims every time we bump into her. "She checked my diaper. I didn't even wear diapers!"

Even though she wasn't quite two years old when said diaper incident took place, Olive still rattles on about the injustice of it all. I listen to her. I make room for the venting. I try to draw out her under-lying emotions. I tell her I understand. I talk about choosing kinder words than "hate." I drop subtle reminders of all the wonderful things about Teacher Janice, all the reasons we chose the preschool, all the special experiences we shared together there. Sometimes, I roll my eyes behind her back. Other times, I giggle to myself or laugh about it with Jeff.

One might question whether there was molestation involved. Since I'm certain that's not the case, it's looking in the mirror and being aware of my genes that helps me understand what's really going on—a pastime I still find fascinating as an adoptee who grew up without the extravagance of genes to study up-close.

I don't have to zoom in very close to see that my poor youngest has inherited my sensitivity. She's attuned to the slightest of details. Her sense of smell is frightening. I may think I'm surreptitiously popping a Hershey's Kiss into my mouth while she's down the hall brushing her teeth, but twenty minutes later she's asking, "Mama, what did you eat? There's chocolate on your breath." I painstakingly cut out the tags from all her clothes, and still, even the pin-striping on a pair of leggings bugs her susceptible skin.

Trickier than moving around her sensory issues is helping to guide her heart, which pays the biggest toll for her sensitivity. This dear child of mine is so easily wounded. Once hurt, it's incredibly hard for her to soften—the necessary precursor to forgiveness.

Olive's bright as a whip and so cognitively understands, on some level now, how prone she is to feeling hurt and how wounding this world can be. In quiet moments when we're talking together, side by side on her bed, our faces washed in a lavender glow from her purple night-light, Olive's smirk tells me she gets it. Still, mention Teacher Janice (or any of the children, teachers, or babysitters who may have cut in line, talked about their playdates in front of her, made her best friend cry, missed something she said or misunderstood her), and she'll launch into her I've-been-wronged diatribe.

When she's that prone to being hurt, the concrete-paved road of anger can be so much easier for the heart to go down than the vulnerable, ethereal path that requires feeling the disappointment and pain, experiencing both the yearning for deep connection and its lack, and then deciding to risk another collision ... by forgiving.

I know.

***

"Why are they laughing?" Mom said.

"They're laughing? In a friendly way?" Amy naïvely asked. "Maybe there's something funny?"

I could read the fear in Mom's face, though, and saw there was nothing friendly or funny about this.

"It's wrong. All wrong," Mom said. Then, as if an ordinary day, the distance in her blue eyes disappeared and she smiled at me. "Cute pants!"

I sighed, relieved that intense moment was over and Mom, who loved shopping and clothes and always delighted in my personal fashion, had returned—to me and to herself. *Let's get back to dropping it,* I thought.

"I need to get back," she said a few moments later.

"To heaven?" I remembered that dying people sometimes feel "held back," as described in the vignettes shared in *Final Gifts.*[2] "Is that where you've been going?"

"What?" She seemed surprised by my presence. My pants were cute, yet she'd already forgotten I was still sitting on the bed next to her.

"Heaven," I said. "You know, where you'll go."

Mom shook her head. "I don't know." She stared through my eyes again, drawn, instead, into that other realm—a terrible, uncertain, pained look on her face.

She'd always been so sure of her faith. Even in her fear of death and desire to stay with her family and see her grandchildren grow, Mom had been excited to meet Jesus and reunite with her grandbaby Kenna. Never had she, or any of us, expressed any doubt about where she was headed. How could she not know, while dying, whether she was going to heaven?

Mom's loss of confidence throttled me. I felt like I was spiraling down a dark tunnel at high velocity. The part of me that had been getting vengeful satisfaction knowing she might be accountable for her lies suddenly felt sick.

Mom just had to be allowed into heaven. I'd never been sure that my mother's religion was for me. But heaven was my bridge, the only chance I'd ever have of seeing her again. I agreed with Mom. *It was wrong. All wrong.*

I wanted her. I needed my mom—imperfect no longer mattered. Just as our adopted dog Peetey's soul seemed akin to mine, Mom's soul seemed to be beautifully matched with mine. Simply put, we fit together.

Had I ever told her that? No, it always seemed too dangerous. Mothers leave. I had to stay guarded, for survival's sake. She wasn't perfect. Then again, neither am I as a mother. But she was my mother. I wanted her ... as much as she'd wanted me.

I prayed. "God, please. Whatever these lies are about, please forgive her. I forgive her. If this is about my adoption, I forgive her and it's okay. Please don't make her suffer like this!"

Forget about any lies that might have been. Lies to me, lies to herself. She had just been immature. It wasn't her fault. She just wanted a baby. Me. She really wanted me. And I want her. In life and in death.

With my prayer interceding between Mom and me, I pioneered my way up the vulnerable path of forgiveness. At last I understood how Mom had to believe in the simplicity of my butterfly story and why she had to make it her own. She was a good person. She wouldn't have been able to live with herself if she thought she'd outright taken another mother's baby—especially knowing that my first mother had wanted to keep me. Mom had to believe the fairytale that my adoption was divinely arranged.

I understood and I forgave. Or I forgave and understood — which came first didn't matter. Hopefully having traveled this path, one day my daughter will learn to forgive, too.

CHAPTER THIRTY

All of You

There is no fear in love, but perfect love casts out fear. For fear has to do with punishment, and whoever fears has not been perfected in love.
—1 John 4:18 (ESV)

In the last few days before her death — at Mom's bedside with Dad and Amy — Mom repeatedly struggled to communicate important things whenever she was awake.

Sometimes her mumbling would make sense. Other times, it left us puzzling.

Urged by a hospice nurse to write down her thoughts when the words got stuck, Mom spent ten painful minutes struggling to write, "I love you."

We gushed as soon as we finally deciphered her cryptic cursive.

"Oh, Mom. We know you love us," I said. "We love you, too!"

How tender, we seemed to think in unison, smiling together as a family — the quintessential moment Lifetime movies are made from.

Mom had more to say, though, and exerted desperate energy trying to write more. Dad and Amy left the room to see the nurse out. With determination, Mom kept scrawling on the notepad while I earnestly tried to understand her scribbling. But she could barely grip the pen in her hand. Sensing her frantic need, I offered a pencil, then, by accident, a straw. *Maybe this fat blue marker will do the trick?* Still, nothing Mom wrote made sense to me. My two preschoolers had better penmanship.

She finally gave up writing.

"All of you." She blurted out loudly. She said it again, the second time pointing to the notepad, where she'd underlined what I could now decipher was "All" written in slanted blue cursive repeatedly on the page. She brightened with relief when I echoed the words back to her, and soon fell asleep.

Deciding she needed my help sharing her dying communication with "all" the others, I ran to tell Dad and Amy.

"Oh, that's so sweet," Amy said.

There was something I wasn't quite grasping, I could tell. Amy didn't even seem all that impressed. But it was obviously hugely important for my mom to get out.

Maybe she meant "ALL of you," as in not just our immediate family? Perhaps someone else needed to hear Mom's message?

With the zeal of a news reporter on deadline, I cranked out an email to "all" our relatives and Mom's wide circle of lifelong friends, passing along "all" of her love. To be extra sure I got Mom's point across, I attached pictures of both her love notes. I even added a P.S. message: "Please feel free to forward along if I've inadvertently missed anyone." All thirty-four people on the distribution list basked in the sweetness of her messages. Mutual love letters back poured in.

After a peaceful night's sleep, the next morning Mom could speak again — mostly in short, fractured sentences that she struggled to get out.

Then, she looked at me, a fierce intensity in her ever-striking blue eyes.

"We're going in circles," she said, frustrated.

"What do you mean?" Amy asked.

Keeping her eyes fixed on me and with bewilderment lacing her voice, Mom said, "You're still not getting it?"

"Getting what?" I asked. "What aren't we getting?"

Then, after a pause, where she seemed to be talking to someone else not physically in the room with us, she turned back to me and said, "We don't know if it's a boy or not."

This wasn't morphine-talking nonsense. In fact, Mom had only been taking small doses here and there, and none yet that day. Mom was starting to make sense. But I didn't like it.

Instantly, I felt like I'd been caught, purple-handed. I might as well have been five years old standing outside the grocery store with a stolen pack of grape Hubba Bubba in my pocket—not a grown woman sitting with my mom on her death bed. It took everything inside me to stay in the room and not run away. I felt myself emotionally numb out, going inward. There was no doubt in my mind that Mom was speaking of the unborn child from my abortion. *Maybe my baby wasn't a girl.*

It overwhelms me to speculate on how Mom knew. As she continued laboring toward death, I kept witnessing her straddle two worlds—ours, and whatever other one lies beyond this place after we die. Repeatedly, she had conversations with people—long-passed relatives? God? Both? Sometimes someone else seemed to be guiding her words.

Perhaps one of these people told her. Perhaps she met my unborn child. Perhaps it was as simple as a mother's intuition and our mutual lack of courage to ever say anything to one another for over twenty years. We mirrored the mother-daughter silence between Diane and Shirley. An intergenerational pattern, across two different families, that in both cases determined a baby's fate.

The moment was loaded with what felt like sacred meaning.

This was the moment of truth, and I was in trouble.

Spending two years in the hot seat of a women's group cult came in handy. Instead of fleeing from my discomfort, I realized it was time to dive into it.

"Dad, Amy?" I cautiously whispered. "Can I have a moment alone with Mom?"

Maybe they'd been ready to flee. They scurried right off, leaving me alone in the room with Mom.

After a few minutes of silence, I decided to open up to Mom. Risking my heart, her disapproval, and her love, I told her my deepest, darkest secret, about the abortion that had taken place almost twenty years earlier.

"I'm sorry for not telling you," I sobbed.

"It doesn't matter," Mom said — a bit too quickly, I thought. I'd waited too long. She was too close to the end to comprehend what I'd just said. Didn't she have more to say about it? She'd always been so vocal about her anti-abortion beliefs. After all, her adoption of me was an anti-abortion success story.

I couldn't stop crying, shaking, apologizing again for not telling her sooner. "It's never felt right to keep secrets from you."

And then, with nothing but love, care, and understanding, Mom gently and clearly responded, "Oh, Sara. Sara. Sweetie."

Throughout the rest of the day and into the night, I felt lighter than I'd ever felt before. And from then on, closer to Mom than I ever thought possible, letting her acceptance and love for me fully sink in — the secrets and division lifted away.

No longer going in circles, at last I understood the dying message Mom had been trying to communicate to me. Sharing my secrets wouldn't break me. Or her. Or our relationship.

Mom loved me.

ALL of me.

Blessed to the Max

By Linda Easterly, to Sara

Wednesday is my adoption class—I have it all written (and it's really good) but I didn't know if you had a comment or a thought. I am showing a Mother's Day card you made if that's OK (with a picture of a butterfly flying away, and you crying, and me pointing toward a church).

It makes me realize all over again how God blessed us to the very maximum you can bless someone when He put you with us! No matter what else happened in my life, that was the best thing (but I'm not sharing that in the class).

Ma

CHAPTER THIRTY-ONE

Making It

They shall build up the ancient ruins; they shall raise up the former devastations; they shall repair the ruined cities, the desolations of many generations.
—Isaiah 61:4 (ESV)

Mom and I began to talk heart-to-heart—that's the best way I can describe it—and became closer than we ever had been before. Even though Mom was lying listless in a different room than mine, I could hear her loving voice talking through me. And she, apparently, could wordlessly hear mine. I wouldn't have called it "telepathy"—that didn't seem descriptive enough. But it was the only word that helped me make sense of it … even though making sense of it didn't matter to me at the time. My focus was on purely delighting in it.

"Close your eyes, sweetie. You should really try to get some sleep."

But the last thing I could do was sleep. Mom was right with me, overflowing with nurturing—exactly what I'd always longed to receive from her. I wanted to keep talking to her that way, letting it lift me up. I worried, too, that she might go away. What if when we stopped talking … she died?

Mom had complete patience and delight in me. "Oh, Sara. Remember our road trips to Montana? How I'd leave in the middle of the night thinking that way you would sleep for the drive? But instead you'd be wide awake, and stay up all night talking and talking and talking."

I had forgotten, and we laughed about it together. My memories from childhood seemed to have been soured by my more recent reflections. Mom helped me remember the good times — which had, to my surprise and delight, been plentiful. Her story reminded me just how well she knew me, too. We had so much history between us. I felt known and cherished. I had my mom back — the mom I had long forgotten her to be. Had Mom suddenly learned to speak in the heart-language I needed ... or was it that I had finally learned to let it in?

As an adoptee, the trauma of an early separation from my birth mother predisposed me to not easily trusting people — especially, ironically, those closest to me. Verrier has explained it this way:

> The severing of the bond with the birth mother has a lifelong impact on adoptees, as well as the mother. It calls into question basic human relationships. This is especially severe for the adoptee because her earliest postnatal experience is that of disconnection from the mother/self. She learns that the world is unsafe, perhaps even hostile. Trust, the cornerstone of all relationships, is destroyed. Mother, the one with whom she was connected for nine months and whom she should be able to trust and nurture and protect her as long as she needs her, has disappeared. How then can she trust anyone else? Connection or intimacy is experienced as a precursor of abandonment and must be avoided at all costs![1]

But adoptees don't own the corner on trauma. "Almost everyone has suffered some emotional trauma during childhood," according to Verrier. "Children are more easily traumatized than most people realize."[2]

Mom had experienced early trauma, too. As a five-year-old, she was left in a hospital for a year. She'd been admitted for a tonsillectomy, but the care team had not checked her for strep throat, first, so the infection moved to her kidneys. Mom stayed in the hospital for a year — during a time when childhood medical workers were uninformed of the impact of separation on young children and so not motivated to keep patients together with their parents. Worse, Mom's dad — my Papa — landed a new job in Hardin that year. The rest of the family moved from Minnesota to Montana, leaving Mom, just a kindergarten-aged girl, behind in the hospital until she recovered. Mom had come by her own attachment and abandonment struggles honestly.

Attaching deeply seemed to be challenging for both Mom and me. Mom had clearly attached with me at sameness — one of the shallower levels of relating — happiest when she and I dressed alike, looked the same, acted the same. I knew Mom could go deeper, into belonging and loyalty, but perhaps she'd gotten stuck at that level. Maybe that's why she took my search for my birth mom as such a threat to her family. According to that way of relating, it would make sense that she'd perceived me as disloyal.

But I'd seen her attach deeply with others — my sister, in particular. I'd always blamed it on not being Mom's biological child, not being loved the same way by Mom. But now I had to be fair in my assessment. I had to believe Mom's words from a letter she'd written to me when I was in high school: "I'm very fortunate to have had the opportunity to have both adopted and given birth. Only I can know that neither way is better than the other."

In that same letter, she'd added:

My love for you just simply can't be measured. Even I am overwhelmed by it. (By the way, I understand that your love for me does not have the same intensity as mine for you. I think I can even accept it.)

God sent me quite a handful when he sent me you. It became apparent very early in your life that you were exceptional. I trust that we'll somehow make it, Sara. I promise you my loyalty, my concern, and (for better or worse) my mothering. I love you.

I remembered my fifth birthday. It fell on the first day of kindergarten. Despite my fierce independence, Mom made sure I had birthday fanfare. In the afternoon, she came to school with a bucketful of tambourines, maracas, horns, and noise makers—enough for each child in class—and led everyone in a parade as they honked and sang to me. Whether she consciously realized it or not, birthdays can be painful for adoptees. My birth had been full of pain and sorrow that my body would never forget. The magic Mom created on that birthday—relinquishment day—and every birthday thereafter, helped counter my sense of worthlessness.

Mom *had* been affectionate. She *had* been nurturing. Not all the time. Not perfectly executed. But she'd tried. She did the best she could—given her own wounds and working around mine.

Verrier has pointedly asked adoptees: "How many of you have felt as if your adoptive mothers were unaffectionate? If you are honest, do you think they just gave up after awhile?"[3]

Mom hadn't given up. She might have been dying in the room down the hall from mine. But she remained right there with me all the same. Loving me. Nurturing me. Believing in me. Knowing, at last, that her faith in us wasn't for naught.

Mom was right. We'd made it.

I wished it hadn't taken so long. I wished Mom didn't have to die for me to let her love in and to feel so close to her. But connecting this deeply was simply too vulnerable until now. Thankfully mother-daughter connections don't end with death. In Mom's and my case, death could only make us stronger—both a tragedy, and a gift.

I remembered a deadline. Swaddled in the surreal experience of Mom and I conversing through our hearts, I'd forgotten about the outside world. It was almost midnight, and I was about to miss an important deadline.

"Sorry, Mom," I said. "I'm supposed to get this essay posted today."

"Yes. Go do it," she said. "That's important."

I excused myself to get the job done.

When I returned, Mom was still accessible through my heart. I felt happy with the essay I'd written, but happier that work hadn't disrupted our connection.

"Thanks for understanding, Mom," I said.

"Just keep talking and just keep writing, Sara. You have so much in that heart of yours that needs to come out."

I did. How did she know? All these years, I thought I'd kept my heart disguised so well. But at the same time, I'd been desperate for her to see it. At last she did.

"Try to sleep now honey." Mom said. "It's really late."

"I don't want you to go, Mom. I don't want you to die."

"Don't worry," she said, "I promise not to leave until you're ready."

Could I ever be ready?

PART III
God, the Mother

As a mother comforts her child, so I'll comfort you.
—Isaiah 66:13 (MSG)

CHAPTER THIRTY-TWO

Calm Before the Storm

Let the peace of Christ keep you in tune with each other, in step with each other.
—Colossians 3:15 (MSG)

I woke up the next morning remembering a conversation with my wise friend Mary. "You're on holy ground there right now," she had told me. "I know it's hard, but try to find a way to enjoy it if you can."

Mary was right. The house seemed to radiate peace, and I enjoyed it immensely. Mom and I continued talking together through our hearts shortly after breakfast. She hadn't gone away while I slept. When I'd go into her bedroom to physically be with her, I couldn't feel her voice anymore. Mom would be reduced to a still and suffering body lying on her bed, waiting to die. But as soon as I'd leave the room, Mom and I were able to talk heart-to-heart again. In spite of the grim circumstances with death looming so close, I felt a new kind of lightness having Mom right there with me, fully accessible like that.

A few of my friends—Mary, included—whose mothers also died too soon had mentioned how they could communicate with their moms after their death. I never questioned their experiences, but I'd found the concept a little woo-woo. Now, though, I understood. Maybe it would be this way from here on out—Mom right there, always with me in my heart. No more phone calls or cell phone charges. Calling plans or death would never touch us. We could talk and talk as much as we wanted. My incessant talking wouldn't even drive Mom nuts, either, like it had on our road trips to Montana.

The house emanated warmth and love. Mom, Dad, Amy, and me spending such intimate time together—just the four of us, like the "good 'ol days" from my childhood. And the more I talked with Mom, the more I continued to remember the good times. In spite of all of my lonely wondering, the stifling of my heart, my silent suffering, my inner turmoil and extended adolescence, it really had been a wonderful family life. Sailing. Laughing and joking—a lot. A tremendous amount of pure silliness. Fawning all over our amazing golden retriever, Sadie. Competing in gymnastics meets and cheering for football games—never an event missed by my proud parents. Close relationships with extended family—beloved grandparents, aunts, cousins—thanks to Mom's dedication to tradition, together with her leadership and organizational skills when it came to sharing Christmases and vacations together. With her creativity and humor, Mom was an outright magic maker. She and Dad had intuitively built a large attachment village for us—full of gregarious sailors, Mom's longtime Bible study friends, Dad's Navy and banking friends, and neighbors who never went away, even when most of us had long since switched neighborhoods. My life had been full of caring adults who'd known me since I was brand-new, when they worked together to hang a jumbo "Welcome, Sara(h)" sign across our house. Almost every one of them had been supporting our family in some way as Mom's death drew nearer ... including my aunt.

I'd called her late the previous afternoon, wondering if Mom was having trouble letting go because she needed her sister there with her—Mom's best friend in the world, plus a nurse and an exceptionally gifted caregiver, too. Aunt Carol flew into town first thing that morning, and now that she was there, it felt like everything had fallen into place. I expected Mom to take her final breaths any time now.

Still, Mom didn't seem ready to go—or maybe it was me who

wasn't ready. Mom said she wouldn't leave until I was ready, after all. And even though I hated that her physical body was suffering, I wasn't ready yet. I wanted to stick around in my parents' house and keep everything just like this. I liked being a dependent child — who knew? I was thriving letting Mom take care of me emotionally. I didn't want to go back to my family in Seattle, to my day-to-day responsibilities, to being a mother of two preschoolers and their monotonous, near-constant needs.

But my flight back to Seattle was booked to leave first thing the following morning.

"I'm going to have to stay here longer," I told Jeff over the phone that afternoon.

"What do you mean?" he asked.

"Well … I promised my mom I'd be here when she died."

Jeff huffed. Or maybe it was merely a pause. It didn't matter. I knew him well enough to sense his frustration. I had taken care of every possible child-related detail for the last four nights to make my absence as easy as possible for him. I'd rallied my own family's "village" to help support our kids while I'd be gone so he wouldn't have to take off time from work. He'd had full support from his parents, our former nannies, friends, their preschool teacher. But he was being put out.

Why wasn't there a generous "yes" from him? If at any time I needed one, now was the time.

"Well, how much longer?" he asked. "I've got a huge proposal to get out tomorrow, a big client meeting Monday. My parents have to get back —"

"My mom is dying!" I snapped. "What kind of question is that? How would I know how much longer? Those things don't even matter!"

Another pause. "Of course, your mom is the most important, but—"

"But?" I yelled. "Hold on ... I need to talk to my mom about this."

"No, don't go in there and wake her up!" I heard the panic in Jeff's voice. Nobody wants a witness when they're acting selfish, especially one who always—ALWAYS—takes her daughter's side.

"I'm not going to wake her up." I braced my fists on the counter as I leaned over the kitchen island. I was so mad I could have lifted the granite slab over my head. Instead, I held on to its edges, hoping its coolness, stability, solidness would seep through me. "I don't need to go anywhere to talk to her, remember?"

I wouldn't be able to wake up Mom for a discussion in her slipping-away state, anyway. She was mostly gone, long-gone now, from her body. Had he already forgotten that I'd told him, just this morning, how Mom and I were now communicating through our hearts? Saying it out loud made it sound sort of silly—delusional, even. But I couldn't deny the real conversations and love Mom and I had been sharing throughout the day.

"You still there?" Jeff asked. "Hello?"

"My mom's right here with me, remember? In my heart. Just hold on a minute. I can't hear her voice when you're talking, when we're fighting like this."

I needed to ask her what to do. I needed to know what she wanted me to do. But I couldn't hear her anymore.

Earlier that spring, when we realized that another lung transplant wasn't going to be an option, Mom and I had talked about her approaching death and wishes. As we'd talked, I'd promised her that I would do everything I could to fly home and be with her during her final moments. I hadn't directly asked if she wanted me there. I just assumed she would need my care. She'd agreed ... hadn't she? I remembered her saying that keeping it to our family of four felt right.

But did it still feel right, now that we were in the thick of it? The more I thought about it, and the longer her death took, I wasn't completely clear anymore on what she wanted.

"How much sleep have you had, Sara?" Jeff asked, concern in his voice. "Maybe you should go try and take a nap."

Oh. The sleep card. A continual marital struggle between us — Jeff still not realizing, as Mom always understood, that my "normal" was running on hardly any sleep.

I shook my head. "This has nothing to do with sleeping!"

Jeff wouldn't let it go. He was worried now, not just about sleep, but my mental state. I wished I could redo my life and not go to that essence restoration seminar, nor come back temporarily unhinged. I wished I'd never given him any reason to wonder about my sanity. But then, would continuing to repress all my emotions have kept me any saner?

Regardless, I didn't want to talk about sleep or sanity right now. I was desperate now to hear from Mom — and not just about whether or not to leave her side and fly back home to my family.

Another question had floated into consciousness as Jeff and I argued. I remembered the mother-daughter memory book I'd just read in Mom's room a few days earlier. In that book, she'd written down all kinds of memories — of her mom, of her childhood, about my childhood, and the woman I had become.

But the page headed, "Mr. Right" ... she'd left that page blank. She'd given me the book when I was in my early twenties. I hadn't met Jeff yet, so it hadn't seemed odd that the page was blank. But just before Violet was born, I'd looked through the book again. I wanted it finished. Jeff and I had been married for five years at that point. Time to fill in the "Mr. Right" page. On my next visit to see my parents, I'd given it back to Mom, asking if she'd complete that page for me.

I'd completely forgotten about the mother-daughter album, hadn't realized that she'd never given it back ... until I stumbled across it on Mom's basement bookshelf the week she was dying. I'd picked it up, sentimentally rereading all of the pages again while keeping her company as she slept. She had written in the book about her dad's death. My revered Papa. I remembered how hard that was for her to be there with him when he died. She never could shake the image of his complete loss of dignity while dying. It was terrible for her, and it made me wonder whether she wanted to protect me from feeling the same way watching her.

But then I turned to the "Mr. Right" page. Still blank. After all these years, she had never filled it out. *Why?* As Jeff and I fought, I looked for deeper meaning.

You don't think he's "The One" for me, do you, Mom? I tried to ask through my heart. *You knew this all along.*

Over the phone, Jeff kept interrupting. "I'm really starting to worry about you."

I set down the phone to shut Jeff out. *Do you think I shouldn't have married him, Mom?*

I couldn't step back to consider that the stress of Mom dying on both Jeff and me had anything to do with our fighting. It seemed like this had to be bigger than that. I had to know Mom's answer!

But I never heard it. My thunderous phone call with Jeff turned into a full-blown hurricane. The storm inside me shifted the connection between Mom and me. I quaked with upset that my heated conversation with Jeff had been so disruptive to Mom's peace and that of the rest of my family, even after I'd moved downstairs.

Worse, though, was realizing that not only had Mom's voice

gone away, but I'd welcomed in a monster I hadn't realized was lurking so close to my emotional edge, just waiting for a chance to rage.

Feeling the loss of the peace, losing my connection with Mom, and feeling my sense of security flee was devastating and alarming. The buildup of all the emotions of the last week while I'd been supporting Mom in her death, combined with the lack of sleep and overwhelming separation I'd had to face — all of it — crashed over me.

I cried.

CHAPTER THIRTY-THREE

Only Me

His mother held these things dearly, deep within herself. And
Jesus matured, growing up in both body and spirit, blessed by
both God and people.
—Luke 2:51-52 (MSG)

"After the relationship with the adoptive mother, the next most difficult relationship is that with a partner or spouse," according to
Verrier.[1] In that moment, I couldn't have agreed more—except that I
might have insisted marriage was harder than any mother-daughter
relationship, no matter how defended its participants.

Now that Mom and I had come to a place of healing and closeness, apparently Jeff came next on my relationship to-do list. I didn't
want him to die for us to "make it," though—no matter how much
residual anger still smoldered inside me after my tears. Still, the
timing was atrocious. This was not the time to be attending to my
marriage.

I'd cooled off a little by late afternoon. But I felt too bitter and
angry, still, to soften my heart and find Mom's voice again. I decided
to reschedule my flight to extend my stay. Jeff would be stressed at
home, but I knew he'd come around to seeing it my way. I had to
admit, he was decent that way. Besides, I couldn't worry about my
husband, or the kids, right now. I had made a promise to Mom, after
all. Jeff could manage. It's not like he was doing anything all that
heroic—taking care of *our* kids for a few days—that I hadn't been
doing every freaking day since they'd been born. Besides, both of his
parents were there helping.

My mother would only die once. I had to be with her, and I couldn't imagine it would be long now before she died. It had been over a week since she'd eaten anything. She wasn't waking up or seeming conscious at all anymore.

I dialed up Frontier Airlines. Something must have gone wrong. Out of the blue, the hold music stopped and everything went silent. I'd been disconnected.

I redialed. Same disconnection again.

I decided to wait. Mom, as well as her funeral plans, needing attending to. I'd deal with the flight change later—after ordering the bulk cinnamon bears (Mom's favorite candy) to be placed inside miniature shopping bags (in honor of her number-one pastime) that Amy and I had dreamt up for memorial service giveaways. Surely the airline would get it together soon, get their phones back up and running properly.

Later that night, after designing a poster-sized photo collage to display at Mom's funeral, I dialed the airline again.

The phone system still didn't seem to be working. I kept getting bounced out. "Press one for new reservations. Press two if you have an existing reservation ..." I listened carefully this time, lest I push the wrong button, trying not to let my mind wander to the many places and thoughts it wanted to stray at the moment while the monotonous robot droned on with menu option after menu option. Finally, I made it in ... only to hear, "Due to unexpectedly high call volumes, you may have to wait longer than usual."

Thirty minutes passed. *Why, yes, that is a longer wait than usual!* I dared not hang up at this point, though. *Surely an attendant will pick up any minute.* My return flight was scheduled for first thing the following morning. It was getting late. I had to get through to someone soon. Starting over in the phone queue wasn't an option.

Another thirty minutes passed, bringing me to the one-hour mark. Still, nobody came on the line to help me change the flight.

Amy, and then Aunt Carol, popped into my bedroom to tell me Mom was okay and they were going to bed.

"Your mom must be behind this," Aunt Carol said. "Or God. You might have to give it up, Sara, and get back home to your family."

I'd been starting to wonder that myself.

"Yeah, well ... then this is the ultimate mother-daughter show-down. I'm going to win this one!" I laughed to channel my most stubborn virtues ... and cover up my doubts. Mom was one absurdly determined woman. *How else would she have survived all that she had? How else would she still be alive right now? Could I really compete with her herculean stamina?*

"Good luck with that," said Aunt Carol, smirking. "I'm going to bed."

Finally, after ninety minutes of listening to hold music, then no hold music, then going through the menus all over again, I hung up. Mom must have had continued assistance from the other side. My earthly powers were no match.

I called my mother-in-law, Willa. Maybe she'd convince me to stay a little longer. Maybe I'd convince her to stay with Jeff and the girls for one more day. If not, perhaps I could talk her into reaching out to one of our friends, neighbors, or teachers for back-up.

"It's great you have all of these people lined up, Sara," Willa said. "And we'll find a way to stay if you need us to."

"Really?" I asked.

"Of course," she said. "But your mom is right. Your family needs you."

Willa's words surprised me. *They ... needed ... me?* But why?

I was just a mom. Doing my mom-job. Doing the things moms

do. Attending to their needs. Reading parenting books. Taking parenting intensives. Organizing their closets. Decorating their rooms. Volunteering in their playschool classroom. Throwing them Pinterest-worthy birthday parties. Walking them through their tantrums. Match-making them to their teachers. Trying to get it all right. Perfect. It had all been just a job to excel at, to master—like all the jobs I'd ever set my mind to. The hardest job I'd ever had, of course. And … I was nailing all the tasks at hand, I had to admit, whether any performance review told me so or not.

But mothering was about more than metrics, more than merely setting my *mind* to it. More than checklists. More than building up an attachment village to replace me. My kids, and Jeff, needed more of me than that.

I remembered Olive at seven months old. I had her bundled in the baby sling so I could hold her close while bustling about, picking up the house. Attachment parenting via baby-wearing—checking that off my list while multitasking—just as I had while nursing Violet and giving myself a crash course in parenting. After finishing the play room, I moved toward the kitchen. Midway up the stairs, Olive reached out and grabbed my chin, pulling my head toward her until we locked eyes. I looked at her and smiled. As soon as I looked away, she did it again. Over and over for months, her soft, wee baby hands pulled my face into hers whenever she sensed my distraction, forcing me to pause and remember her. Her determination, her desire for connection with me was a surprise.

I never wanted to believe any of it had anything at all to do with me. I was replaceable, wasn't I? *Mothers are replaceable, yes?* Hasn't that always been common knowledge, deep down in my psyche, reaching all through my body, too, even down to my bones? I was a mother who'd been left by my mother—and still just an unlovable, unwanted, broken child inside. I was never meant to be marriage material, let alone motherhood material.

Only … my birth mother had not been replaceable. If Diane had been, I never would have bonded with her in utero. I never would have spent my lifetime longing to find her. I never would have pressed on so doggedly to find her.

Even though being replaced was her biggest fear, Mom wasn't replaceable, either. If she had been, I never would have spent my life trying so hard to take care of her, to do right by her, to endear myself to her. I wouldn't have tried so hard to ensure I'd never lose her.

I finally understood that I was unusually rich in mothers. I could no longer deny how important mothers are. I knew that I mattered as a mother, too.

Again, the words from Mom's letter said so much: "I'm very fortunate to have had the opportunity to have both adopted and given birth. Only I can know that neither way is better than the other."

Similarly, how very fortunate I've been to have had the opportunity to have both an adoptive mother and a birth mother. Only I can know that neither is irreplaceable.

As the sugar on top, I had an intuitive and wise mother-in-law in my mix, too.

I considered trying Frontier Airlines again. But I had to trust that the powerful trifecta of Mom, Willa, and God knew a lot more about mothering than I possibly did, no matter how much knowledge I had acquired. It was time to go home to Jeff, to Violet, and to Olive.

I would leave on the flight the next morning. I would not be at my mother's side to comfort her during her final breaths. I wasn't Mom's caretaker anymore. It was my young distorted thinking that it had ever been my job in the first place.

I had a real job now. I had to learn to depend—and accept the caring being offered to me — so that I, in turn, could care for my own family.

They needed me.

Only me.

CHAPTER THIRTY-FOUR

A New Lifeline

God allows storms in our lives to teach us to pray.
—Pastor Richard Dahlstrom[1]

Just as I climbed under the covers that night, a loud and ferocious thunderstorm swept over the house. Not a tornado, but another of my most formidable nightmares: an angry storm at bedtime. Thunder cracked and shook the floors of the house. Barberry shrubs outside spread their arms, flashing the windows with their thorny silhouettes with every burst of blinding lightning. The storm seemed so fierce, so intense, and it had moved in too late at night, in my opinion. *While Mom was dying, no less!*

To distract myself from the intense fear, I decided to read the latest draft of Mom's public testimony, *Butterfly Heaven*. I'd drummed it up earlier that day while preparing for her funeral. Whether I disputed the details or not, Mom treasured that story and the sharing of it. I'd talked it over with Dad and Amy, and we'd decided it would be honoring to include it in the program.

In really being open to it, rather than half-listening as I always had before, I finally understood how aligned Mom and I were—symmetrical, almost. Our mother-longing. Our fears of abandonment. Our needs to express ourselves through writing. Our desires to be known. Our abilities to believe in the sometimes unbelievable. Our wishes to become the answer to our daughters' needs.

I come from her, too.

As an infant, I'd lost my sense of self at the very time I lost my birth mother. But my mother/self was being reborn now. I didn't feel untethered anymore.

I felt my bitterness lift away, realizing that it didn't matter whether Mom had the details about my butterfly story precise. The story didn't belong exclusively to me. My story was a part of her story. Her journey was a part of mine. We'd been perfectly knitted together — by thick roots that had grown out of our individual histories, memories, and perspectives. Weathered and aged but growing deeper still, our roots braided to form one masterful story of far-reaching, sustaining growth. A story of a mother and a daughter. The story of us. An imperfect mother and a broken daughter — held together in the rich soil of love.

Perhaps it was the lightning that scared me into a state of dependence. Perhaps it was feeling another wave of grief over how long it had taken me to fully attach to Mom. Perhaps it was the almost unbearable separation I couldn't escape, knowing Mom could die any moment. Out of the blue, I felt inspired to read the Bible.

As soon as I had this thought, I knew that Mom had left one for me in that guest room.

Where is it!? Where'd you put it, Mom?

I opened up the nightstand drawers. Nothing. Then, I saw her antique desk in the corner.

I paused for a moment, scared of what I already knew would be inside. With trembling hands I opened up the desk.

There it was — a tiny, slightly tattered New Testament. Mom's first Bible. Somehow I knew it had been left there for me, left there for this exact moment. Ironically, the precise size and shape as my iPhone that is almost always in my hand as if a lifeline to the world.

A new lifeline?

I didn't know where to start. For a minute, I just stared at the list of books, hoping for guidance as if I held a flattened Magic-8 Ball. *Matthew, Mark, Luke, John, Acts, Romans* ... I realized that the order I'd memorized in Sunday School at Ridgeview Hills Church was coming back to me — whether I'd been the one to snag the candy prize, or not.

Frankly, I'd always found reading the Bible boring. It would put me right to sleep. And sometimes Mom would make mention of certain things from Revelation, and it would utterly terrify me. I wanted to steer far, far away from that creepy, hell-and-brimstone-sounding stuff.

But that night, while thunder rattled the windows of my room and preyed upon my familiar somatic storm anxiety, as Mom continued dying in the room above mine, I shakily opened up to Revelation. I didn't understand much of what I was reading, but this line stood out: "I am the Alpha and the Omega."

I closed the Bible, then realized that Mom's voice, which started talking with me again earlier that evening, had changed. It was a different voice, and it struck me that it had been sounding less and less like Mom as the night wore on.

Confused, I asked, "Wait a minute. Who is this? Mom? Me?" *Shoot*, I thought, *have I just been making this all up? Am I losing it?*

But labeling myself as crazy was another byproduct of being adopted, of having so much intense emotion swirling around inside before I had words or conscious memory to make sense of it. "Babies already 'know' about adoption. It happened to them," explained Verrier. But without context for the loss, "they often feel abnormal, sick, or crazy for having those feelings and puzzled by their own behavior."[2] It was time to shed that inaccurate belief about myself. Just as Mom and I had believed in the supernatural visit from my Papa so many years ago, my instincts told me to trust in the mystical now.

"God?" I tentatively asked, "Is that ... you?"

I thought back to those childhood Bible camps, how I'd followed the counselors' precise instructions to invite Jesus into my heart. I'd never felt anything change. I hadn't felt anything at all, except awkward discomfort and self-consciousness. Surely, I hadn't done it right. More surely, God wasn't interested in messed-up me.

But had God been there, anyway, unbeknownst to me?

"You had to attach deeply to your mother," God said through my heart, "And first, before attaching to me."

Without further words, I understood. I had to learn to deeply love another—in my case, Mom—to trust in her spirit of unconditional love despite its sometimes-flawed attempts, to accept all that she gave me instead of focusing on her faults, and to truly let it all land. Only then could my heart soften enough to find and trust God.

But where had Mom gone? Was this a trade—Mom, for God?

God assured me that Mom wasn't going away, but that he was going to take up the biggest place in my heart.

God stayed there with me, soothing me throughout Nature's sensation outside.

Finally, the storm began to grumble onward. Instead of covering up with a pillow, I rested my head on one.

It made sense. Giving myself safety from the storms wasn't possible. It was something I could never give myself. It wasn't something Mom could give me, either.

Only God, my new lifeline, could calm my storm fears.

And just like that, he did.

CHAPTER THIRTY-FIVE

Alpha & Omega

You're blessed when you feel you've lost what is most dear to you.
Only then can you be embraced by the One most dear to you.
—Matthew 5:4 (MSG)

Dr. Neufeld often talks about alpha—being alpha to our children, and the great fulfillment that gives us as parents when we can set aside our own needs to provide for our children more than what they are asking for in order to bring them to rest.[1] He has spoken of God as the ultimate alpha, which is why I couldn't get that scripture from Revelation out of my head. "I am the Alpha and the Omega."

When I first heard Dr. Neufeld describe alpha dynamics, even though from the perspective of parent, I couldn't help thinking of myself. I'd learned that a lot of my instincts to take care of Mom were driven by attachment. It was my brain's own fault for deciding it wasn't safe for me to depend, one of the main causes of an alpha complex.[2] From a psychobiological perspective, I'd missed a "crucial relationship event," as described by Thomas Lewis, M.D., Fari Amini, M.D., and Richard Lannon, M.D.: "A mother and her child are meant to be together postpartum, when their neurochemistries are busy weaving the ties between them."[3] Like all brains, mine had been designed with great purpose. It hadn't falsely perceived danger. My trauma was real. My brain erected defenses that were necessary for my survival. And they worked! But over the long-term, they also kept me stuck, even if I'd come by that stuckness—that I'd previously coined "baggage"—honestly or not.

Learning about attachment dynamics not only made sense of my stuckness, but it also shed light on the second main cause of an alpha complex: failing to encounter a strong alpha presence in the primary working attachment.[4]

When I first learned this, I felt angry, and sad, wishing Mom had been more alpha to me. It wasn't entirely a response to the adoption trauma my brain had responded to. It really often *had* been my job to care of Mom's emotional needs.

Even from the start, by the fact of being adopted, I was an answer to Mom's need (and my dad's, too). By adopting me, Mom could fulfill her desire to become a mother. The setup was focused on *her* needs, not mine. I had, after all, a birth mother and birth grandmother who'd been prepared to raise me had patriarchy and my parents' needs not intervened. My birth mother, who was a legal adult shortly after my birth, went on to raise three children, the first of whom was born less than four years later. Diane became a capable and strong mother. Mom wanted to become one, too.

As I grew up, my emotional needs, specific to being an adoptee, were not fully attended to. Verrier has explained:

> If the adoptive mother fails to be told or fails to believe that her child is aware of the differences between his two mothers, she will be missing an honest connection with her child in favor of a myth — that it makes no difference to the child who the mother is, that he is not aware of the absence of his first mother, that he is not grieving. She will be unable to be attuned to him, to soothe him, and to help him regulate his emotions about this terrible experience in his life. He will be unable to find a way to truly connect to her.[5]

Even though prevailing adoption wisdom taught no better, it wasn't sound logic that Mom could simply and uncomplicatedly replace my birth mother. She didn't look deeper, and my brain perceived that

Mom didn't have the alpha presence I needed to walk me through my emotions or to help me make sense of them. Like Evan voiced to Amy, I unconsciously said to Mom, "I take Sara's hand." *I'll be the one in charge of the caring.*

And then, while I was still in my extended adolescence, Mom got sick. Over the twenty years she lived with polymyositis, and even more so after her lung transplant, the number of drugs Mom had to ingest became exponential. Many of the drugs had nothing to do with the disease—just additional drugs to combat nasty side effects of other drugs. I watched Mom become weak, hypersensitive, increasingly insecure. Her bones broke easily. Her face and body swelled, and she felt self-conscious about these changes. She had mood swings. She began to struggle with anxiety and depression. Most people applauded the way Mom fought back with humor, her steadfast faith that God had everything under control, and how she'd eventually pull out of her "funks," as she'd call them. I admired her strength and courage in that way, too. But those of us closest to her also sometimes felt the impact of the disease and its side effects. I had grown older, but I hadn't altogether grown up. I was unwilling to take Mom's disease seriously and therefore couldn't impartially judge the side effects, which I instead took as proof that Mom wasn't alpha enough for me, proof that I was the strong one who had to stay in charge.

But the last two days had saturated me with memories of Mom's immense caring: her complete devotion to our family; her absolute and pure delight in her children and grandchildren; her infusion of humor and fun; all of the creativity she poured into our home; all of the loyalty and love she and Dad valued and shared; all of the senti-mental ways she collected details about Amy and me to be sure we had the keys to understand ourselves; all the ways she taught us; the values she instilled in us to give us the foundation for a strong faith; how she not only poured her heart out through story, but always encouraged the storyteller in me, too; all the numerous ways she put Amy and me first—our needs ahead of hers. As it turned out, I had been raised right—only it had nothing to do with whether I shared my parents' Swedish or German heritage.

Mom gave me so much—and more—in all of these areas that I could take it all for granted and find rest in her generosity. That's exactly what being alpha is all about: providing more than is being pursued. In fact, so much more, that it can be completely taken for granted.

In the last twenty-four hours, I'd witnessed Mom transform. She'd become fully alpha, filling in the gaps that she couldn't earlier, whether due to her illness or her own shortcomings. While in the midst of dying, she had found a way to take care of me, my marriage, my children, and my spirituality. She gave me love. It may have been imperfect before, but it didn't matter now that she'd learned exactly how I needed it, and I'd learned exactly how to receive it. Though she had bravely faced death and looked forward to meeting Jesus, reuniting with her dad and grandbaby Kenna, Mom decided she wasn't going out from this world until she had everything in order, until she could rest knowing that I was being taken care of. As she'd assured me over and over while we conversed through our hearts, "I'm not going to leave until you're ready."

What I didn't realize as she told me this was that she wouldn't be ready until she transferred the attachment from her to God—the ultimate Alpha. God was the only way she could take care of me in her death, the only way I'd be protected from my fears, and the only way to satiate my hunger for a completely unconditional invitation to exist—just as I am.

You Are My Child

By Linda Easterly, to Sara

Dear Sara,

As long as you live, I'm going to be your mom. I have always and will always love you more than anyone else in the world. I know you know because you're a mom, too.

I can't ever become your friend even though we are friendly ... because I choose to remain your mom. Not a mom with expertise, just a mom with a ton of love.

I've gone through a really tough time since you found Diane. That's because I don't want to share you. But I've come to realize it is me that you've had forty years of sharing a life with ... through frustration, fights, and the ultimate amount of pride and joy. Nothing can undo that connection.

As your mom, I understand what you needed to do. I think knowing Diane will complete you in the one way I can't.

If I say things wrong, or feel ways you don't appreciate, it is ok, because what I won't let you down on is ... being there for you ... every time, believing in you ... every time, (but not necessarily seeing things the way you do every time).

You are the child I've thanked God for. You are my child.

Love, Ma

CHAPTER THIRTY-SIX

I Felt the Light

God will be your eternal light, your God will bathe you in
splendor. Your sun will never go down, your moon will never fade.
I will be your eternal light. Your days of grieving are over.
—Isaiah 60:19-20 (MSG)

I should have fallen straight to sleep. Saying goodbye to Mom,
attending to her funeral plans, had left me exhausted. But the closet
was on my mind now ... or, more accurately, on my eyes.

In the guest bedroom at my parents' house, I always leave the
closet light on, the door ajar just enough so that a wee sliver of light
leaks out into the room. It helps me fall asleep. But in the midst of
the raging storm, I'd needed more than a sliver. Now light beamed
into my eyes, making it even more difficult to sleep than it already
was—even with my storm fears calmed, knowing Mom might die
any moment wasn't conducive to slumber, either.

"You don't need that light," I heard a voice through my heart.

"What?" I stopped myself from wiggling further down into the
covers to shield my eyes from the bright closet. I hadn't realized God
planned to stick around.

"You don't need that light," God repeated. "Use mine."

Flicking off the closet light wasn't something I would have done
on my own, nor at the prodding of anyone else. Over the years Jeff
has certainly tried weaning me off the night-light, to no avail.

But God suggested it, and, well, it felt like I should listen.

So despite my wishes and through my fear of the dark, I got back
up and turned off the closet light. Then I dashed back into bed, afraid

to have my back to the dark closet any longer than necessary. I faced the closet door and studied the darkness, as if a child again, on the lookout for a dragon to pop out.

God assured me that it was okay to close my eyes, that I'd still see the light.

I closed my eyes.

"Can you feel it?" God asked.

Yes. Yes, I did. There was God's light! But it wasn't coming from the direction of the closet. The light was aglow somewhere in the back of my head, it seemed — so bright that I could feel its warmth inside my body.

I opened my eyes, then rolled over to peek if there was a car driving past the window or if the light was coming from something similar: headlights, streetlights, lightning. *There must be a rational explanation.*

But, no. It was nearly midnight. The suburban streets were quiet, the storm had finally subsided. I couldn't see a hint of streetlight glow in the bedroom, either. The entire room was dark. Darker than I'd ever allowed a room to be — at least while I was in it. *How was the light coming from the back of my head? And how was I seeing it? How did its heat emanate and warm my entire being?*

Like a scientist needing evidence for my hypothesis, or a modern-day Doubting Thomas, I decided to run another test. This time, I closed my eyes while facing the window instead of the closet. I still saw the light. I still felt the light. Its illumination came from the same place, as if inside the back of my head, only now the back of my head was aimed at the other side of the room, confirming for me that the light wasn't coming from the street.

My own personal night light! I thought. *Well … this is great!*

I flipped over again, concentrating on the glow inside me.

A part of me still couldn't help wondering if I was imagining God. Pablo Picasso once said, "Everything you can imagine is real." By that logic, God talking to me was real. God's voice and cadence were so unlike mine, and I didn't think I was imagining the light. But even if I were, wasn't God the one who gave me my imagination? Every time I'd taken my daughters to the aquarium and marveled at all the unusual shapes, colors of rare sea creatures, I'd seen proof of God's wild imagination.

I stopped analyzing. God really was with me. I could feel God's light. "The light was good. And God separated the light from the darkness" (Genesis 1:4 ESV).

God's light inside my head was bright and warm and white. Science lessons teach us that white light is made up of all the colors of the spectrum: red, orange, yellow, green, blue, indigo, and violet. Rainbow light. *I'm always chasing rainbows.*

"You're not alone," God reassured me. "I'm here."

"We are not alone in this world, nor have we ever been, no matter how much we may feel otherwise," wrote Dr. Diana L. Hayes, author and professor emerita of systematic theology.[1] But I'd always felt alone … until now.

God proceeded to show me how I've spent my entire life feeling alone, unsafe, and scared-to-trembling not just of natural disasters and the dark, but also of roller coasters, down-escalators, spiders, fires, burglars, unlocked doors, school shootings, my children dying. It became clear how I'd been working overtime to try and protect myself. Because I didn't believe anyone else would, I had to stay fiercely vigilant.

God helped me see how our family has always had a history of trouble sleeping. My grandma, Mom, Aunt Carol—they've all struggled with insomnia, and Restless Leg Syndrome, which created more insomnia. I'd always felt fortunate for not inheriting their sleep problems. After all, I'd reasoned, I sleep so incredibly deeply once I finally do go to bed—even if by the time I go to bed, there are only a few hours of sleep to be had. But for the first time, with God lovingly showing me something Jeff had been complaining about for years, I could honestly look at what was now clearly fact: I've always had trouble sleeping, too. Mom had just reminded me how I talked the entire eight-hour drive from Denver to Billings—even when she drove us there in the middle of the night in hopes that I would sleep.

"Even when you were a very small child you didn't need a lot of sleep," Mom had said recently, after I'd complained about how Olive wouldn't go right to sleep at bedtime. "So I'd just let you play quietly next to me until ten at night." Apparently, that was easier than fighting with me for hours and hours to go to sleep.

God was right. I had a sleep problem, too—sleep avoidance. And all at once, I remembered how I was always scared of falling asleep, of nightmares ... but then how scary it was being the last one in the house to fall asleep, as a result. A no-win situation of gripping anxiety. Loneliness. How it seemed as though the darkness could swallow me whole. God showed me that from the start I've been in a desperate fight to keep my eyes open, to keep myself always totally busy—in an incessant struggle to keep myself safe. Not only was the night-light required, but I'd work late into the night and wake up early. I would avoid sleep and darkness as much as possible without spending summers in Alaska where there's daylight for twenty-two hours. *If I see it coming, whatever it is, it can't get me.* But now I knew it wasn't working.

I understood how my survival tactics weren't cutting it. Each day I only feel more and more unsafe. And because of my lack of confidence, I'd been inadvertently passing along many of my fears to my children, as well.

"Everything is going to be okay," God said. "Just use my light."

"You wonder about a lot of illogical things when you are adopted," wrote author Deanna Shrodes.[2] None of this felt logical, but I couldn't deny that for the first time in my life, my fears were put to rest.

Mom's human shortcomings no longer mattering, I gently fell asleep in the warmth of God's glowing light.

And that light was good.

CHAPTER THIRTY-SEVEN

A Time to Laugh

A time to weep and a time to laugh; A time to mourn and a time to dance.
—Ecclesiastes 3:4 (ESV)

The next morning Amy dropped me off at Denver International Airport. We hugged on the curb, ignoring the bossy overhead voice reminding us to stop only long enough to load and unload. We both knew that by unloading and walking into that airport, I wouldn't be there when Mom died. I'd be breaking the promise I'd made. Even though I knew how to find her in my heart now and could remain with her that way, I'd still be leaving Dad, Amy, and Aunt Carol alone to care for Mom as she took her final breaths.

But the matter wasn't in my hands. I had ceded to what felt like Mom's wishes to protect me from the gruesomeness of death's final moments. I accepted that God didn't seem to want me there, that my husband and children needed me back. I had to accept it all.

When I got to the terminal, I felt God talking to me again, telling me to go buy an eye mask from the airport convenience store to help me sleep on the plane.

Do they even sell those things anymore? My mind flashed through decades, wondering when I had last noticed someone wearing one of those—in the nineties, perhaps? *Wasn't that just a passing fad for people to wear those things on trips?* Of course, I kept myself too busy, usually, to pay any attention to other passengers.

I looked up. There, right in front of me as I stepped off the escalator, was one of those airport stores that sold everything from news-papers to bottled water to mass market books to an array of Denver Broncos souvenirs. *Might be interesting to check and see if they have eye masks*, I thought. *Maybe I hadn't really heard that.* Not to mention, after four nights of not sleeping very well, listening to every nuance of my mom's stuttered breathing as her oxygen tank shook the ceiling above my bed, getting a little "shut-eye," as Dad would call it, sounded kind of nice.

As soon as I walked into the store, I spotted an eye mask. Just one left, in fact, dangling on display from a shiny silver hook right in front of me. In any other state of mind I'd find this a little creepy. Maybe it was the writer in me, ever interested in a good story, but I found it sort of fun playing this out. I grabbed the eye mask and took it to the counter to pay for it, then stuffed it into my carry-on as I walked to my departing gate.

When I arrived at the gate, an attendant announced that the flight would be delayed due to mechanical problems.

What?! I panicked. *What if the plane goes down? Mom and I will die at the same time.* For a flitting second, the thought brought relief. *I'd love to go with her.* A part of me had been jealous while watching her journey back and forth from earth to heaven. I wanted to go to heaven, too! There was too much suffering here. Wasn't that why I'd always secretly yearned to die? Why thoughts of suicide as an escape had always seemed so alluring before?

If Mom and I die at the same time, I won't have to feel the pain of her leaving.

Then I remembered Jeff. Mad at him as I still was over the previous day's phone call, I'd never see him again. Violet and Olive … who'd be there to help them grow up? *They can't lose their mom. They really do need me.*

God kept talking to me, telling me to trust him. "This is going to be hard—the greatest separation you have ever faced in your life, leaving your dying mother. But I'll be there with you the whole time."

"I'm going to die now, too, aren't I?" I asked.

God assured me he would never do that. "That's not how I work in times like this."

I could have flipped back through memories of news headlines, stories I'd heard, urban myths. Surely, that sort of thing had indeed happened before. But I didn't. I chose to believe God.

Once the mechanical problems were finally announced as solved, I apprehensively boarded the plane. I felt on the verge of a panic attack at several points while waiting for the other passengers to board. I thought about getting off the plane. I could picture myself responding to interviews later, after the plane went down, telling the story of how I just missed a crash by intuitively not getting on board. But I was ignoring my own intuition now. God assured me again and again that he wasn't going to leave me. "Just put on the eye mask."

As the airplane doors closed, I pulled out the mask from my carry-on, wringing it in my hands while considering whether I'd really do this.

"Keeping your eyes popped open like you always do isn't going to keep the plane in the air," God told me. "Only *I* can keep it up in the air."

He's kind of arrogant, isn't he? I pondered. Which I found sort of funny. *Why shouldn't he be arrogant? Um .... he's God.* I guess because of being God and all, he not only came up with Bernoulli's principle before it was named as such, he'd also noticed how I always sat in the window seat and kept my eyes fixed on the runway to scan for possible danger as if I were the pilot's way-backseat assistant. I hadn't consciously noticed that about myself before. But God was right, and I had to chuckle. God wasn't laughing at me, but he made me laugh at myself.

Okay, then, I'll play this out, I thought. *What have I got to lose?* I put on the eye mask before the flight attendants finished their safety announcements.

As the plane taxied on the runway and then lurched into the air, I marveled just a bit. I couldn't believe I was doing this—not keeping watch. Later, when I felt turbulence, which in the past always filled me with dread, God said, "See there, can you feel me rocking you to sleep?"

I smiled. It never occurred to me to think of turbulence as a soothing matter. But yes, I could feel it now.

Then God jauntily added, in a voice and vocabulary that made it clear it wasn't my own: "Besides, just so you know, the pilot is a believer." I laughed. Did I really care whether the pilot was a believer? Did I even like the term "believer?" These weren't things I'd wondered about before, really. Or if I had, it elicited my eye-rolling. I hated that sort of Christian-speak. But I had to admit, it gave me comfort thinking of God and the pilot working on the same team. I kept the mask on and kept talking with God.

He was quite a character, God.

"By the way, you've got to stop sitting in these seats in front of the exit row that don't recline," he said. I smirked, having been caught again. I've always told myself I like to stay busy on the plane, so why bother reclining? But God was on to me.

He reminded me again about the believing pilot. Then, in an off-hand, almost flip way, he added, "And if that's not enough, there are a lot more believers flying with you on this plane."

I got excited at that, feeling like the princess I always knew I was destined to be. It's the Hebrew meaning of my name, after all. *A full escort service, just for me?*

Reading my mind, God said, "Yes, but don't get too cocky about it. They're here for others reasons, too. I'm working all of you on this plane right now for all different reasons. But if you need them, they're here."

There was nothing to do but laugh at his high-and-mighty sense of humor, his casual-yet-important air. *Working all of us ... really?* Not what I would have expected ... but then, why not? God couldn't be funny?

The plane continued to coast toward Seattle. Mom could very well be dying right then. I was flying farther and farther away from her. Yet getting to know God in this very personal way that reframed all of my previous learnings about a sinless man who bled to death on a cross—whom I'd therefore surmised must be serious and boring—well, it just kept cracking me up. *How could it be?* And to find out God knew me so well, too ... well, it made me giddy inside.

It should have felt wildly inappropriate. And yet it felt so right, I knew it was my time to laugh.

CHAPTER THIRTY-EIGHT

Looking Up

Beloved, let us love one another, for love is from God, and whoever loves has been born of God and knows God.
—1 John 4:7 (ESV)

When I rose from window seat 9A to head for the bathroom, God told me to look up and try to spot the believers.

But, I thought, *who were these "believers," anyway? What did that even mean? Would I really know them?*

I walked down the airplane aisle, pondering each person who met my eye, and realized it felt strange to look people in the eyes. Had I really never had the courage, or interest, to do that before? Only two days earlier, I'd read a note Mom had written long ago, reflecting on how extremely shy I was as a child, how painful it was for me to make eye contact. Mom and I both thought I'd outgrown that tendency.

But, as God helped me see, I hadn't.

❦

Tijuana, Mexico was a scary place to visit—at least when I was seven. It wasn't rumors of crime, drug cartels, human trafficking, or homicides causing me to fret, though.

It was my hair.

My blonde hair, draping the sides of my face and obscuring my downcast eyes, drew too much attention in Tijuana. I'd become so used to looking down, hiding myself, that I wasn't aware of this handy security tool until it failed me in Mexico: Eyes down first, followed by my curtain of hair to keep the overwhelming world at bay. No eye contact required. No looking my fears square in the eye.

But I couldn't stay hidden in Tijuana, where children both younger and older than me reached out to touch my nearly platinum strands. Shopkeepers nodded their approval at it. Leering teenaged boys addressed me, "Hola, Blondie!"

I stood out like an orphaned fawn in a vast, open meadow. As an adoptee, I had an aversion to standing out. Adoptees "don't want to stick out too much and we don't want to offend anyone, so we learn the cultural patterns, rules, and mores of whatever culture we find ourselves in," wrote Verrier.[1] It was just a day trip. There was no time to immerse in the culture. So all day I refused to speak, not wanting anyone to notice that Spanish wasn't my language. And I most definitely did not look up.

Whether on vacation in Tijuana or back home in Colorado, it was as if the whole world held the brutal power of the blazing sun over a hot desert. I couldn't stare at its people directly, lest I get burned.

Depersonalized, nonhuman attachments became my best friends. As a child, books helped pull my eyes downward, into the whimsical world of make-believe with favorites like *Charlotte's Web* and *The Chronicles of Narnia*. I had gerbils, teddy bear hamsters, and ferrets to cuddle in my lap at first—and later, my golden retriever and constant sidekick, Sadie—drawing me into the furry, non-rejecting animal kingdom. Then as an adult, I poured myself into my career, and my smart phone—that glorious gadget I could turn to whenever I needed to get out of an awkward moment, feign importance, or drum up work for myself to ensure I never paused for a breather ... or a proper look.

Never consciously considered, but an instinct always at the wheel—that drive to stay focused on another activity or world apart from this one. Keep that veil of blonde-turned-brown hair wrapped around me so I could hide myself, ever looking down or eyes flitting around, afraid to land. Safer than having to look directly at this terrible, scary world.

As I looked up at people flanking the airplane's aisle, I saw many eyes smiling warmly into mine. *Try to spot the believers*, God had said. As I smiled back at my fellow passengers, I found them. Words weren't needed to feel our connection together. It was clear as the cerulean-colored sky outside us that we were connected to each other. All through God.

A woman, about Mom's age, stepped out of the bathroom right as I arrived there. As we awkwardly maneuvered the tight hallway, she warmly put her hand on my arm and held my stare, smiling at me.

It felt like a dream. *Why would a complete stranger cross my personal space to hold on to my arm like that, for no reason? Did I have a notice on my forehead: "Be nice to me. My mom is dying right now."* The bathroom mirror proved otherwise.

She must have been one of God's believers.

But what about the others? They seemed nice enough. In fact, as I stepped out of the bathroom, I felt a connection to every person on that plane.

I thought about my Muslim friends. My Jewish friends. My agnostic friends. Even my atheist friends. Sure, I had Christian friends, too. But more of my friends *weren't* Christians than were. Some of my life's most remarkable memories and pivotal points had been lived with many of them. What about the women from the women's group?

Two Buddhists, a closet Christian, an Atheist, a Unitarian, a Science of the Minder, and a handful of generally spiritual women walk out of a women's retreat together ...

While I'd felt a pull to envision Rebeca as my long-lost birth mother, what had initially drawn me in was the fact that no matter our faith, we all wrestled with the same issues. The women's group helped break me away from my own self-focused landscape, revealing to me that we all shared the same existential concerns. Underneath our varying spiritual beliefs, we all wore the same themes of our humanity.

I'd never wanted to embrace a God who decided that certain people were "in" — presumably, the "believers" — and everyone else was "out." I'd always felt like I was out, anyway.

But had it actually been God making me feel that way?

On the contrary, God was holding me right now, clearly showing me that I was "in."

Maybe we're all "in," but we're too quick to believe the lies. Lies whispered from our wounded places of abandonment and rejection telling us we're broken. Distortions we internalize when we compare and contrast ourselves with others who look like they have all the Bible verses, and life, figured out. Lies that tell us to keep our truths hidden in the dark because surely they'll destroy the façade of love we never truly deserved.

I was in. I walked back slowly to my seat, relishing the chance to study all the seemingly kind people who appeared to be looking back up at me. We're all in.

As Dr. Diana L. Hayes has written, "This is our calling as Christian faithful: to recognize the Christ in everyone."[2] Kelley Nikondeha put it another way — a way that resonated when I thought about the connection I felt with all of these people, and also between Mom and me: "We are connected by more than genes; we are relatives by daily fidelity and even deeper mysteries."[3]

I basked in the comfort of knowing God's people were among my allies right then. But even more mind-staggering was pondering how God was doing all of this — "working" all of these people at once, as he had called it? *Was he talking to my mom right now, too, like I now understood that I had witnessed just the previous day? How many others were dying at that very minute? How many other daughters needed God soothing them? Was God with all of us at once, mothering us all?*

I could not stop marveling at the mystery of it all. But I knew the answer was yes.

Rebuckled in my window seat, I realized that I'd never felt so safe while suspended in an airplane in the sky. I didn't have the urge to look out to be sure the pilot had everything in order. Earlier, I had even boldly shut the window shade! But God guided me to open it up, to take a look.

"I made all of this," God said in this proud way I still wasn't quite used to. "Yes, the world can be very scary and you have not felt safe here. But I made all of this. It's beautiful, too."

The sun shone brightly on the landscape below us. As if for the first time, I really took in the deep canyons, lush evergreens, huge snow-capped mountains, vast skies — the clouds, rivers, immense sky. The view really was astounding. *Maybe it isn't the horrible place I've always thought it was.*

"See? It's really beautiful ... and I need believers to make it that way."

How could I argue with God, looking through that lens? Hadn't God given me glimpses before? When I held my niece Kenna in my arms for the first time and felt her inherent goodness? After my laser eye surgery when I realized how much care and detail went into each and every pine needle? The time we watched the baby turtles embark from their nests and lumber to the ocean?

And that day I was a young, carefree child skipping along after my butterfly friend. That day the driver didn't bother to brake for her, hadn't looked up over the steering wheel to see my friend's flawless wings flutter so gracefully in the summer sky, moments before the windshield crashed into her tiny body. *What kind of person doesn't notice beauty, right there in her face?* I'd judged.

I wasn't meant to be someone who blindly rushed through the world. Though I understood her now.

I wanted to see beauty again, and love. I wanted my vision corrected — permanently, this time. It was time to start looking up.

CHAPTER THIRTY-NINE

Writing Mr. Right

Relish life with the spouse you love each and every day of your precarious life.
—Ecclesiastes 9:9 (MSG)

While I seemed to have God's undivided attention, I decided to ask about Jeff. Mom hadn't answered me the day before, after all, when I'd urgently asked her whether I made the right decision by marrying him. I still wondered whether she'd known something I hadn't.

"Why did she leave that page blank, God?" I asked, "Is Jeff not 'The One' for me?"

For so much of my life, I'd been accepting whatever gusts came my way—had Jeff just been a gust I said "yes" to marrying eleven years earlier, simply because he'd asked?

"Why don't you pull out the book," God suggested.

What? My eyes drifted to the carry-on in front of my seat where I'd stored the book, *To My Daughter, With Love: A Mother's Memory Book.* I hadn't wanted to risk losing it with my luggage—the record of Mom's musings on my life, which she had poured her heart into back when I was just twenty-four.

"What do you mean?" I asked, full of fear.

"Go ahead," God said to my heart. "Pull it out."

Seriously? My mind raced through all of the miracles I learned about in those Sunday school classes. God had parted the Red Sea. Fed thousands of hungry people one time from a couple of fish, right? Hadn't one of the disciples walked on water? And how about those people who saw the Virgin Mary's face in their pancakes?

I imagined myself opening up the book and turning to the "Mr. Right" page. Yesterday, it had been blank. Mom, I knew, was too close to death to have completed it. I remembered her childish handwriting, "<u>ALL</u> of you," and how challenging it had been to decipher. Besides, the mother-daughter book had been in my possession ever since I rediscovered it. *No, there's no way she could have filled it out.*

Had God filled it out for me, though? What if it was in Mom's handwriting? What if she'd done it supernaturally? First, talking through my heart ... and next, filling out a book for me? Now that my curiosity was piqued, I almost couldn't bring myself to check. I might not be able to handle the disappointment, or any more losses that might follow. *Would Jeff's name be there? What if it was someone else's? What would I do then?*

"I'm not supposed to test you," I said to God. Though I couldn't recall the specifics, I remembered something like that from childhood disciple stories. But still ... how cool would that be? To open up the book and right there, on page 64, find my answer ... God's very own answer! *Never again would I doubt whether Jeff was the man for me!*

With jittery hands, I leaned over to pull out the book.

"Really, God?" I asked. "Should I really open this?"

"It's okay, yes. Go ahead," God said. "Open up to the page you're wondering about."

Cautiously, I flipped past "Then There Was You." I thumbed to "When You Were A Little Girl," then came to "First Wings" — the section about my first day of school. In Mom's elegant loopy cursive, in black ink, she'd written, "The first day I was prepared for your hysterics. Instead, you took off your little sweater and said, 'Go home now.'" I'd been pushing away care, deciding I could solely take care of myself, for a long, long time. As with all the other pages, Mom responded to the prompts with descriptive prose and family photos that precisely accompanied each subject.

Finally, just after the "When We Became Friends" spread, I land-ed on the "Mr. Right" page.

Blank. Just as it had been yesterday.

I knew better. I had tried not to get my hopes spun up … but, still …

"See, there, you were testing me," God teased.

"I know," I laughed. Still, I felt so disappointed. Crushed. *Why couldn't the page have been filled out? Everything would be so much easier that way.*

"Now take out a pen," God said.

"What?"

"Fill it out yourself."

"Me?" I asked.

"Your mom wasn't able to do it," God said. "But you can fill it out now, just as she would have."

Again, it hit me just how unwell Mom had been. Of course, she would have filled out the "Mr. Right" page for me. She'd never expressed any qualms when I'd returned it to her and asked her to complete it. In fact, she'd always adored my husband, whom she fondly called "Jefferson."

How had I forgotten our StoryCorps conversation from only one week earlier? Dad, Mom, Amy, and me sitting in my parents' living room for what turned out to be our last family conversation while Mom was still coherent. As Mom went through the list of conversa-tion starters I had printed off from the StoryCorps website, she had said, "My real goal for you is that you stay married. 'Cause I think that's hard. Really hard. There are so many times you go through not wanting to be married for a while. Not being in love for a while. Not even likin' him. And to get through all those times is hard. It'd be real easy, even more than for us, to get divorced. But that definitely is a wish, that you won't be."

How quickly I'd forgotten Mom's answer to the question, "Who's been the most important person in your life?"

"Dad," she'd said to me—as in my dad, her husband. Her "Mr. Right."

I'd forgotten about Costa Rica. Jeff and I took our first vacation together there. On our first morning, Jeff had spotted a butterfly, larger than my hand, that had landed on my back. The butterfly held on to me, riding piggy-back for the photo op as I gleamed into the lens, delighting in nature, Jeff, and brand-new love. The butterfly, which I later identified as an owl butterfly, seemed to be posing for the picture, too, showing us its spotted owl eyespot on the underside of its wing. At the risk of over-spiritualizing, perhaps it had been a sign. Butterflies often seemed to lead me in the right direction.

Then, I remembered what happened only two nights earlier ...

I'd been lying in bed downstairs, directly underneath my parents' room, unable to sleep as I listened to the sputtering rhythms of Mom's oxygen tank. Fighting sleep, I strained to hear hints of voices muffled through the floor, or sense footsteps overhead to signal activity. Mom wasn't awake much anymore, and I wanted to be with her every moment that she was. Surely my vigilance could protect her from one of her greatest fears about dying: suffocating. Mom was scared she might literally choke to death.

It wasn't long after midnight when choking and gasping sounds roused me. *I must have fallen asleep on my watch!* I whipped my legs out of the covers and ran upstairs.

Expecting the moment had come, I was shocked to walk into my parents' bedroom and feel radiant love emanating from inside the quiet, still room. My parents both slept soundly, facing each other on the bed, their heads touching. Their bodies and legs had curled up toward each other. Together, they formed the shape of a heart. Together, my parents were modeling the very symbol of love.

I couldn't help but stare at this intense, and yet subdued, demonstration of their affection.

I hadn't really witnessed love like this. It caught me off guard. I wanted to stay longer and take a picture. But feeling like an intruder, I went back downstairs to bed.

Mom had been sick. So very sick—from her disease, from the drugs that were fighting the disease, and from the drugs that were fighting the drugs that were fighting the disease. She'd been sicker than I'd ever been willing to look at, didn't want to see. Too sick to complete the "Mr. Right" page in my book when she'd been so swept up in enjoying the time she had left as Grammy and Mom. The page remained blank, but Mom's legacy of wisdom said it all.

So instead of being the reader of our mother-daughter book, I became a collaborator. Writing from my mother's perspective, I pulled out a pen from my purse, which just happened to match Mom's black ink. I began to write, surprised by how easily the words she would have written flowed onto the page.

I turned to the "Your Wedding" page. Under the headline, "What I Wore," I recalled Mom's soft teal dress and how it lit up her ever-sparkling blue eyes. But mostly I remembered her overjoyed demeanor that day. It wasn't just her eyes. Mom herself lit up the room. Instead of describing her clothing, I wrote: "the biggest smile I'd ever worn."

All these years I'd been searching for Mom. "The One" and only Mom—the mother who I knew could give me the comfort and unconditional love I knew I deserved. My searching led me to find

Diane, and then to a deeper level of love with Mom, and ultimately, then, to God, who knew me completely and loved and invited me, anyway. My story was never about finding just "The One."

I'd expected Mom to be perfect. I fantasized about my birth mother, wishing Madonna, Rebeca, and anyone else I admired would reveal themselves as my flawless mother. I never found that perfect mother. So I tried to become her myself, for my own children.

Every one of us failed.

God the Mother, though, did not.

God the Mother had pursued me. Rescued me. Understood me. Knew just how to comfort me. Discerned exactly when and how to make me laugh. If there was such a thing as "The One," God the Mother, it turned out, was who I'd spent my life searching for.

Had I been holding Jeff up to the same lofty ideals I held for my mother, and for myself? Expecting him to be flawless? Tallying all of his imperfections? Looking for proof that would rule him out so I could search for a better, perfect husband somewhere else? Wishing my mother or God would spell it out and show me Jeff was "The One" — my "Mr. Right?"

"The assumption is that there is someone just right for us to marry and that if we look closely enough we will find the right person," wrote Stanley Hauerwas. "This moral assumption overlooks a crucial aspect to marriage. It fails to appreciate the fact that we always marry the wrong person."[1]

Trying to figure out if Jeff was my "Mr. Right" was a setup for failure. Mom was never perfect. Jeff never would be, either. There is no such thing as the perfect mother or a "Mr. Right." My longing for that kind perfection, I realized, is simply a reflection of my preeminent yearning for God.

I finished filling out the book and then returned it safely to my carry-on. I checked the time. We'd be landing soon, and I couldn't wait to get back home to Jeff and his imperfect love.

Reflection of Ten Years

By Linda Easterly, to Sara and Jeff

2003. A wedding on the lake
Two young kids, with a new life to make.
They shared some tofu, some leeks, and some rice
To make their futures strong and nice.

Sara didn't know what a kitchen was yet.
And a bigger challenge she'd never met.
She read some recipes and tried some meals
Occasionally learning how failure feels.

The directions she learned to carefully follow
And soon the meals you could actually swallow.
Now ten years after she's an amazing cook
And much admired for the patience it took.

Jeff joined the Iron Man contest that year.
Of failing that challenge he had no fear.
He ran, biked, and swam, and all that motion
Was done when his ribs were actually broken.

The day after Christmas in Cape Coral, Florida
Sara laid in bed feeling just horrida.
So I went to the store and bought her a kit
The results of which shook them up a bit.

So nine months later comes the beautiful face
Of a precious baby named Violet Grace.
Then 15 months after, as it happens
Our Olive Eleanor joined the Alpens.

First a tiny bungalow was bought
And big dog Peetey joined their lot.
But too much stuff and rooms too few
Soon was changed for a house with a view.

Their second dog, Lucy, is tall, not wide
A great big woof with a sensitive side.
This family believes in playing outdoors
But gives it up when Seattle pours.

Just one little decade yet how can it be
That these were just kids back in 2003.
Good luck and God bless you for many more years
As you travel your new and exciting frontiers.

CHAPTER FORTY

Saving the World

I've told you all this so that trusting me, you will be unshakable
and assured, deeply at peace. In this godless world you will
continue to experience difficulties. But take heart! I've conquered
the world.
—John 16:33 (MSG)

Somehow the young woman sitting next to me in seat 9B seemed completely unaware that I had been engrossed in a two-hour conversation with God the whole journey from Denver to Seattle. Maybe she was like I'd always been, keeping herself too busy to look up and pay attention. Maybe it looked like I'd been talking to myself, and she was simply extending me some grace by pretending not to notice. Maybe, since it was all happening through my heart, nothing looked all that bizarre. Or maybe we all look a little odd sometimes, and nobody finds it unusual anymore. Maybe making space for a little crazy is what faith is all about.

Either way, I was so enthralled with God that only once or twice had I briefly considered how I must have looked. But when I did think about it, I couldn't help wondering about the homeless people I'd judged before—the ones who were always talking to themselves on the streets. Perhaps they weren't all cuckoo, either. Maybe they were just conversing with God, too, not giving a rip what the rest of us thought. God's close to the broken-hearted. Why wouldn't God be talking with them, comforting them, mothering them? Like God was mothering me. I wanted to start mothering those homeless people, too.

Flight attendants walked the aisles asking everyone to hand over our garbage, and God seemed to read my mind again. "I love that you're always trying to save the world," he said. But, in the funniest added, "Forget saving the world. I'll do that."

According to Jeff, he first fell in love with me the day I made him pull over. We were about to drive onto the highway, headed toward the Cascade Mountains for a hike. But I'd spotted a ladybug on the windshield. It would never survive the high speeds of Interstate 90, so at the first chance I hopped out of the car, carefully offering my index finger in order to help the tiny spotted bug migrate to a safe blade of grass. As Jeff watched me from the other side of the windshield, it was as if he'd been peering through a window straight into my soul.

It surprised me that the gesture left such a mark on Jeff. I'd been saving creatures all my life, after all. Besides, often *they* were the ones who'd been saving me, gifting me the opportunity to brazenly express caring, love, devotion — not always a safe practice on creatures of the human sort, but vital for heart health ... and good practice, too, for learning to love deeply later.

While living in Colorado, I spent summers rescuing prairie dogs from bulldozers and urban sprawl. After I moved to Washington, my rescuing energy went toward helping struggling writers, and next — rescuing children through various parent education ventures. Over my life I'd relocated countless beetles, flies ... and, when feasible and not too daunting, spiders. I'd helped reunite dozens of stray dogs and cats — and one parakeet — to their owners. A few times, by accident, I even "saved" an off-leash dog or three without realizing their owners were jogging eight feet away. I had the rescuer/helper complex nailed.[1]

"That's *my* job," God said to me. "Stop meddling in my business."

We both chuckled. His direct wit still caught me by surprise. But then I felt ridiculous. *Had I been screwing up God's plans?* That time I spooked the stray dog I was trying to save ... he bolted away from me, leaving a quiet neighborhood road for a busy street as he darted headlong into traffic. He could have been killed. Thankfully, all the cars stopped and the dog ran back home — to my horror, not far from where I'd first spotted him. That was just one easy example. How many other times had I gotten in God's way? The answer, I knew, was embarrassing.

God assured me not to feel like I'd done anything wrong. "You're supposed to try and live in my image. But all of the frantic saving you're trying to do in every corner of your life is up to me."

"Okay," I said, still feeling a little foolish.

"Get out of my way, basically," he joked, turning the moment of shame into an opportunity for play.

I had to laugh again.

"Your job," he said, "is to give your two daughters the same foundation your mom gave you, so that they can give their hearts to you."

I nodded — at least in my heart I nodded. Again, the woman in 9B didn't seem to notice.

"And when they're ready, they can give their hearts to me," God said. "That's the most important thing you can do right now."

The important work Mom had done. Her life's greatest work, perhaps, and she had succeeded. Long ago she'd won Amy's heart. Finally, she won my heart ... and now God had it, too. She had arrived as a mother. The doubts she felt as a brand-new adoptive mother as my Papa teased about me as a crying, grief-stricken infant, the worries that dragged on her heart while she sensed me searching for other mothers — vanished. She was Mother with a capital 'M.' My all-caps MOM.

I missed her. *Why does she have to go? How long has she been suffering, waiting for me to give her my heart?* Sadly, I knew the answer was for much longer than the last week while she'd been dying.

I remembered Dr. Neufeld's words. "It's not about how deeply we are attached to our children, but how deeply they are attached to us. We need them to attach deeply to us in order to keep them close."

It made more sense than ever now. What could be closer than Mom and I being together forever through God?

God said he brought me to the Neufeld material four years earlier, in order to give me the words to understand all of this ... to lead up to this very moment in time, when I'd really need it the most — to give me the guidance and understanding I'd need for this greatest separation I'd ever faced in losing Mom. God was the one who'd been talking to me through the parenting material — in the way that he knew would work best for me.

I thought again about Revelation. "I am the Alpha and the Omega."

I was happy to cede my alpha complex to God ... to stop focusing on saving the world, and instead setting my mind to winning the hearts of my kids. It may have sounded simplistic, but if each of us did that — raising soft-hearted kids who truly *cared* and were unafraid of loving deeply — maybe saving the world could be as simple as that.

Surrender

By Linda Easterly

Oh Lord I surrender to you this day
All my decisions and words that I say.
I'll do what I think you've chosen for me
And instead of arguing, I will agree.

Help me in this endeavor now
Cuz it's unnatural for me to bow
To your commands and your ways.
But it's your name, Lord, I choose to praise.

I'll need your help tomorrow again
To recognize and run from sin
So help me surrender my will to you
And take my heart to fill anew.

CHAPTER FORTY-ONE

Footprints

I have made you and I will carry you; I will sustain you and I will
rescue you.
—Isaiah 46:4 (NIV)

Mom first shared the *Footprints in the Sand* poem with me when I was
a teenager:

> My precious child, I love you and will never leave you
> Never, ever, during your trials and testings.
> When you saw only one set of footprints,
> It was then that I carried you.
> —Margaret Fishback Powers

Mom had returned home from a shopping excursion and placed her
latest treasure—a plaque with the poem printed over a picture of
a beach at sunset—up on our family room mantle. Mom teared up
when she read the last lines aloud to Amy and me: "When you saw
only one set of footprints, It was then that I carried you." As it did
for Mom, the imagery that became almost ubiquitous in evangelical
circles touched me, too. But, like most of her religious-themed musings where I could sense an agenda she had in mind for me, I feigned
disinterest ... then tucked all thought of it into the recesses of my
flatlined spiritual mind.

While I've rarely been to the hospital and have never broken any
bones, I've had so many brushes with death that I've almost lost

track. I'll admit there's some exaggeration in referring to them as brushes with death. Sliding-door moments is probably more accurate. But looking back through my life from a different vantage point, and thinking about the way God rocked me so gently on the airplane to forever reframe my experience of turbulence, it did make me ponder the footprints.

When I was ten, driving with my family from Colorado to Montana for Christmas, we got stranded in the infamous "Christmas Eve Blizzard." Forty inches of snow fell, and winds up to fifty miles an hour whipped across the plains. Deep drifts of snow nearly buried our sedan as we parked, and sat immobile, right in the middle of Interstate-25 just before the border into Wyoming. Every thirty minutes or so, Dad got out of the car to brush off the snow from the windows and exhaust pipe. Over the course of many hours he'd turn the car on for a while, and then off again, trying to strike the right balance of heating up the car, and saving enough gas to warm us up again later. Eleven hours later, in the pitch darkness of night while temperatures were dipping down toward forty degrees below Fahrenheit, we were rescued by a mysterious man driving a snow plow. The truck's blinding lights seemed to arrive out of nowhere. He pulled up behind our car, helped us clamber into the tall seat of his truck, then drove us out of there, to safety. We missed Christmas while holed up in an emergency roadside motel. It took days for the snow to melt enough to finally retrieve our car, but Amy and I didn't mind because the two double beds were like trampolines to jump on, flip between, and fight over. Mom often speculated that the snow plow driver was our guardian angel, only later letting on how grave our situation had been until the anonymous snow plow man saved us.

Years later, while also driving through Wyoming for a family vacation, our van caught on fire. We'd pulled over on the highway so Dad could check, for the umpteenth time, why the vehicle kept giving us trouble. I lifted my eyes up from my V.C. Andrews book to peer out the backseat window. Flames rose out of the gas tank only inches from my face. I smelled searing metal and watched Dad violently flap around to put out the fire that engulfed his forearm. As with the blizzard, help arrived. Two men with industrial extinguishers seemed to show up out of nowhere to help Dad douse the fire. As soon as the blaze was out, they disappeared in their semi-trucks without so much as a, "Wow, that was weird!" conversation, leaving Mom wondering again at the possibility of guardian angels. I was in high school then, and a skeptic—especially skeptical of Mom.

"Well ... it might be a stretch to call them guardian angels, Mom," I pointed out. "They're probably just truckers sharing the road with us who happened to be Good Samaritans."

"Same thing, isn't it?" To her, a rescue was a rescue and a gift from above. Certainly without their help, our blazing Ford van, with two boiling gas tanks spurting out hot fuel only inches from the exhaust pipe (a problem that earned a recall and class-action lawsuit later that year), had likely been only a minute or two away from exploding ... and sending us, along with our propane- and gasoline-filled sailboat, up with it.

There were other close calls. The time our sailboat's engine and sails were both compromised in a storm, and our boat, miles from Florida's coastline and drifting farther away, was almost swallowed up by six-foot waves ... the time a horse I rode got spooked by lightning and I dangled off his flank, helmetless, as he charged straight down the mountain in a panic.

What about my "death wish" phase throughout high school and college? When I seemed to do outrageously stupid things as if hoping something terrible would happen to me? The time I drove eight friends, all stuffed into my Volkswagen Bug, and distractedly ran a stop sign through a busy intersection? All the parties I bolted from late at night without telling anyone?

I was reckless and, I always assumed, sort of lucky. But was there more to it than that? I'd never looked back to analyze the footprints in my wake. How many sets were there? How often was I being carried? Had God been there carrying me all along? Maybe it wasn't just something he came out to do while Mom was dying, but had been doing from the very start, even when I cried all alone as an infant, wordlessly suffering the loss of my birth mother whose voice I couldn't find.

I had never bothered looking back because I always seemed to be okay. And yet, it was disappointing being okay. A part of me had wanted to die, to escape this harsh world. But the part of me that didn't, didn't want to be okay simply because of my own dumb luck. I wanted to be okay because I'd been rescued. Gallantly. Lovingly.

I had a longing in my heart to be saved. While wandering alone in the dark from a party, I'd wonder about dying. I'd entertain thoughts about what it would be like. Then I'd ponder whether my birth mother might happen to live in the house where an attacker would find me. She'd come out to save me, of course. If not her, then a (good-looking) guy would happen to swing by and get me, instead. When I was lost in New Orleans, I called Mom. But she was too far away to help, not to mention that once I'd called her, she became consumed with worry — loving, but not gallantly helpful.

None of them could rescue me — at least not in the way I longed to be saved. Whether they tried, and when they didn't try, it didn't matter. I always felt unfulfilled and eventually ashamed. Ashamed of my actions. Ashamed of my neediness. Ashamed of what so many would have considered my grossly "anti-Christian" past: suicidal ideations, drugs, premarital sex, an abortion, a cult. Ashamed of my whole being—someone obviously unworthy of ever truly being saved, starting from those helpless infant cries in the first bleak hours and days of my life.

Until I sat on the plane, feeling much like the Samaritan woman probably felt when Jesus knew her entire "unholy" past, yet chose to dignify her with conversation and love. She mattered. I mattered, too.

Mom was still dying. I was the only one flying away from her. When I'd first gotten onto that plane, I couldn't help feeling like an outsider, the adopted child who wasn't there with her while her blood relatives were.

But God was there with me.

Why, though, was God with me? Why not my ever faithful sister? Even without factoring in all the shame, my adopted brain couldn't help but compare to the biological one I'd always assumed was loved more. I loved her more myself. She was an undeniably lovable person. Mom's death was hurting her, too.

According to author Kelley Nikondeha:

> Jesus holds deep compassion for all the relinquished ones because he, too, carries this body memory within his own human skin. Whatever his experience of being let go, whether a biting pain or a faint sting, we will never know. But residing somewhere within the body of Christ is the fact of relinquishment and the capacity to comfort us in places when we feel shut out, left out, or pushed out.[1]

Besides, unlike the sibling-like tension in the women's group as we all fought to be favored, God didn't play favorites. God could be in all places, with all of the hurting ones, at once. I put my "unwanted sibling" chatter on mute. The chatter had become irrelevant.

Like the day that Kenna died, I felt an immense and rare love in the midst of unbearable tragedy. Somehow Mom dying felt both grim … and special. Because for the first time, I felt worthy of being saved — because I was being saved. God was there to rescue me.

"See there, can you feel me rocking you to sleep?" God had said.

If Mom had said it, I probably would have laughed or dismissed it in some way. I wouldn't have let it in. If Jeff *hadn't* said it, I would have added it to the list of ways he let me down.

But God was saying it. To me. God, who surely had countless important things to do, was taking care of *me*.

God had always been taking care of me. Only I hadn't ever looked back to see.

CHAPTER FORTY-TWO

Next-Best Thing

Make this your common practice: Confess your sins to each other and pray for each other so that you can live together whole and healed.

—James 5:16 (MSG)

Reflecting on my family and winning the hearts of my kids, I realized I had something else that I needed to write. Pulling out my laptop, I began typing a letter ...

A Letter From Mom
By Sara Easterly

To my unborn baby, I am sorry.

I am sorry that you know I am raising Violet and Olive. That I said *yes* to them. But I said *no* to you.

I'm so very grateful that Diane brought me into the world. At eighteen, she was much more courageous and selfless than I was at twenty-three, when I knew that I was way too immature to be a mother. But then again, so was my mom, as I'd so aptly pointed out to her as a ten-year-old. And immature I remained, even when I finally embraced motherhood at thirty-five ... just as I still am today ... though I hope at least *some* progress is starting to show. If I had known then how motherhood grows us up, how life grows us up, how the continuum of maturity stretches onward until we die and finally transform into God's ultimate vision of perfection, perhaps I would have put more heart into my choice.

But I was too consumed with my own preservation at the time. Neither finding a family to adopt you or raising you on my own seemed viable. My heart stayed out of it.

When I learn from other adoptees' stories how common it is for us to struggle with relationships and with faith, I wonder if you are lucky you weren't adopted like me. Perhaps I've saved you from a lifetime of suffering. But then I remember that despite my suffering — often *because* of my suffering — my life has been complex and rich, full of wonder and love. Because I know sorrow, I also know joy. *There* is the love in the story of a butterfly that suffered and died. The story was never only a tale of suffering. There was also the jovial tour of all the shrubs. Taking flight and taking in beauty — again and again, in spite of any pain mixed into the story. And it was about the mystical and powerful connection between the butterfly and me — two of God's small creatures, who it turns out weren't irrelevant at all.

There are days when I feel sure I saved you for other reasons. Days when I can't find inside myself the mother I yearn to be. Days when I snap at Violet and Olive too much. Days when I don't have patience, the presence, the right words, enough energy. Days when I'm too distracted. Days when I work too much, push too much, meddle too much, or don't push and meddle enough. Days when there's too much yelling, not enough loving. These are the days I think I've saved you from the mess of me.

But as I watch Violet and Olive grow, I see that somehow they are emerging as really amazing human beings — both because of me and in spite of me ... and often, it has nothing to do with me! I'm thankful for God, now, to both show me the way and make up for my weaknesses ... just as he did for my mother, and her mother before her — and even battle-axe Grandma McPherson. I look forward to the day when my weaknesses finally fade away, when I am perfected and transformed. Just like my mom.

As my mom's first child, I helped lead her to God. As my first child, you helped bring my searching to God, too, when Mom opened both my curiosity and my heart by suggesting, "We don't know if it's a boy or not." I don't know if I'd guessed right that day on the mattress whether you are a girl. Or if Mom was giving me an insider's clue that you're a boy. Either way, I'm looking forward to the ultimate gender reveal when we are finally able to meet.

I celebrate that Mom won't leave all of her grandbabies behind when she dies and goes to heaven. She'll not only have Kenna, but she'll have you, too. I celebrate that you'll have Grammy. And, you have God. God, the Mother.

You have me, too. Like my broken childhood watch, which still sits on my writing desk, you are cherished. You have not been tossed away. I didn't know you were in my heart. But you always have been. And you remain there. Now, and forever.

Just as we have free will to accept God or not, we have free will to choose our mistakes. Sometimes we choose them without thought. Sometimes we choose them without our hearts. But we can't live this life without making mistakes.

Mistakes of all kinds are messy. Mistakes are painful. Mistakes hurt—often others. My mistakes hurt you, and all those who haven't had a chance to know you. But mistakes help us grow. Mistakes offer us the opportunity to transform.

My mistakes led me to God. A God who not only forgives mistakes, but also has the power to make every mistake work for something good by the end of the story.

While we're on the topic of forgiving mistakes, maybe Mom hadn't been so far off in her *Butterfly Heaven* story. My butterfly friend had died. There is no doubt in my memory. But no matter how many times I corrected her, Mom persistently kept the storyline the same. Maybe it's because that innate spiritual awareness we're all born with never did leave Mom. Maybe her wise, spiritual side was referencing more than the physical. Maybe the butterfly's soul really had flown away. As in most mother-daughter conflicts, maybe Mom and I both had it a little bit right.

One day my soul will fly away, too. I'll be flying to God the Mother. I'll be flying to my mother. And I'll be flying to you — to finally and fully embrace you ... as your mother, as your next-best thing.

Until then, I have my work cut out for me here. My heart's work: to stop seeing myself as broken, to believe that I truly am motherhood potential, and to follow Mom's enduring example to become an all-caps MOM for Violet and Olive. I won't be perfect. I won't try to be God. But for all three of you, I'll be your next-best thing.

CHAPTER FORTY-THREE

Flying Home

God doesn't come and go. God lasts. He's Creator of all you can
see or imagine. He doesn't get tired out, doesn't pause to catch
his breath. And he knows everything, inside and out ... those who
wait upon God get fresh strength. They spread their wings and
soar like eagles.

—Isaiah 40:28-29, 31 (MSG)

The plane began its descent. I had almost made my way from Denver
to Seattle. The familiar waters of the Puget Sound shimmered up to
the sky, welcoming me back in hues of gold as the city came into
view and the morning brightened to day. I no longer felt like a drifter,
floating along wherever the winds might take me. I didn't sense a
storm I had to flee. Everything seemed right.

"I'm not going to leave you," God told me. "But I won't be talking to you this way all the time."

"Oh ... " I said, deflated. "Really?"

Before I had time to register further disappointment, God added,
"I'm still here and now you know where to find me ... but you've got
to be functional, too."

I nodded, thinking again about some of the homeless people I'd
seen. How tempting it would be to just sit around conversing with
God all day long, if only I could. *Did I have to be functional?*

"And by the way," God added. "Stop resisting your mother-in-
law. What she told you on the phone last night was true, when she
said *you're* the one they need."

I stared out the window, soaking in God's beautiful world and
the brilliant green hues of Seattle on a sunny, June day. It felt more
and more right the more we approached, and then hovered, over the

runway: Leaving my Colorado home, my mother ... to return to my Washington home and the family who called me Mother.

As soon as the wheels touched down, I turned on my cell phone.

"How's Mom?" I texted Amy, fully expecting to find out she'd died while I'd been airborne.

"She's still here," she texted back. "But she's at peace," A harpist would be arriving soon to play soothing music for my mom. The house, I gathered from Amy's description, felt holy once again. *I guess all is exactly as it should be.*

We queued up to deplane. "Are you still there?" I asked God. It had been quiet for a while.

"Yes," God said. "I told you I'm not going anywhere."

"Okay ... um ... just checking."

"I'll always be here," God reassured me. "I'm not going anywhere."

I knew God was still in Colorado with Mom, too. I thought, *What a relief to know he's standing in for me,* or, more accurately, to know that I'd been freed from trying to stand in for God.

Filled with peace, I breezed through the terminal—speeding, now, toward Jeff and the girls. I'd missed them so much, I realized.

I remembered Mom gushing many times over: "Family is what matters most." I'd never fully understood her passion. The irony must have unconsciously puzzled me, since the broken bond from my first family had never been recognized. But that generational wound—another that affected both my first family and adoptive family—would stop with me. Now I wanted to gush, too. I recalled what Mom had said the week before to Amy and me, in response to another one of the StoryCorps questions: "In the end, what matters is family. You need to cherish them. If that sounds old-fashioned, it is. But it's also real. You've got to treat them like they're the most important people ... 'cause they are."

After unpacking, I spent the day cherishing my family, just the four of us.

Shortly before dinner, we went swimming. I held up Violet's legs in the pool while she showed off her latest trick, an underwater handstand. Olive and I faked a tea party on the pool's bottom, and before long Jeff and Violet joined us.

We swam. We played. We laughed.

A time or two I wondered about stopping. *I shouldn't be enjoying myself right now. I don't have my phone with me. Dad and Amy won't be able to reach me. What if Mom's dying right now? How would I know?*

But Violet interrupted my fretting, calling out to me from the pool ledge.

"Catch me, Mama!" she sang out. "Catch me!"

Catch her heart, I felt.

"That's the most important thing you can do right now," God had said earlier. "Give your two daughters the same foundation your mom gave you, so that they can give their hearts to you."

"I'm right here, baby!" I called back to her. Then without trying to be God, I borrowed God's words. "I'll always be here. I'm not going anywhere!"

Violet leapt into my arms, creating a splash that reached all the way across the pool and over to the lap lane. I spun her around, glided her over to Jeff, then turned around to throw my arms up toward Olive, who'd been boisterously waiting for her turn to be caught.

That's when I felt Mom. Noticing me.

Why doesn't she want me? Why hasn't she come to find me yet? Am I really that terrible? Why doesn't she notice me?

I'm getting launched in the air in a football stadium. Soaring, up fourteen feet into the sky.

Mom was there … noticing me. She'd always been noticing me.

Catch me, Mama! I may as well have been a squealing five-year-old all that time. *Catch me!*

At long last, I'd spread my wings and soared like an eagle. No, a butterfly. A butterfly chasing after a rainbow.

Mom caught me.

God caught me, too.

Epilogue

The stories we tell with our lives, then, aren't meaningless absurdities, tragic in their brevity, but rather subplots of a grander narrative, every moment charged with significance, as we contribute our own rifts, soliloquies, and plot twists to the larger epic, the Holy Spirit coaxing us along with an ever-ebullient, *And then? And then? And then?*
—Rachel Held Evans[1]

My story isn't over. I've not "arrived" yet as a mother. My children are older now, and each day only gets harder. The physical load gets less taxing, but the emotional ante goes up with their age—especially as they become their own people, and I feel the conflicted mix of joy and pain when my separation-sensitive soul is triggered. Each day I appreciate Mom a little more—grateful for her patience, inspired by her playfulness, yearning for her steadfastness and wisdom as I tumble along with each new stage of my daughters' lives.

Mothering asks a lot of us. As an adoptee—just as it is for all who've been wounded, and who hasn't been?—I've found it's an ongoing struggle to keep my heart soft. I will likely have a lifelong battle with fear, anxiety, anger, and distraction. I will probably always find it difficult to trust, cede control, and depend. Neither God nor belief in my capacity as a mother have been a quick fix. But I continue to aim there, accepting the care God brings to me through Jeff, other family members, dear friends, therapists, pastors and parenting experts, others in the adoption community, authors, thought leaders—and a menagerie of adorable pets who wholeheartedly accept my untamable rescuing instincts.

For whatever reason, God has also placed into my life a large number of adoptive parents. Many of my close friends are adoptive mothers. It could just be the odds. Adoption touches 100,000 million Americans, after all.[2] But I don't believe it's random. I believe these mothers offer me a chance to learn adoption from another angle. Through these mothers I get to better understand adoptive mothers' perspectives. I can look at their experiences more objectively, less judgmentally. It doesn't feel quite as personal. That's not all they have to offer me, of course. But it's a thing. A substantial thing—perspective. And opportunities to continue to forgive Mom as new layers get revealed. I hope that in turn, my raw and honest perspective offers something to the adoptive parents who've found their way to me.

Though I'm thankful my sensitivity and empathy led Mom to God, I do not concur in the view that I was brought to my family with the sole purpose of turning them into Christians. To me, that's an overly simplistic view of religion—and frankly that kind of perspective has always turned me off of Christianity. It discounts the loss that was and is very real to me as an adoptee. It discounts the very real loss for my birth mother and birth grandmother—as if only one family's triumph is what matters to God, as if the lifelong consequences for my birth family don't matter. But I do believe that God uses each of us in innumerable, multifaceted ways to impact each other on this very deep, meaningful, and wonderful journey we're all on. It's not about an individual's sole purpose, but about how each of our collective circumstances, accumulated and spread over lifetimes, are part of a grander narrative. God's work is massive, and each of our unique stories are complex and intersect more than we realize. It's unfathomable (and not my business, frankly) to consider all of the ways we're woven together as part of God's larger story. And somehow, through the pain or on the other side of suffering, in the end it's all good. As the Apostle Paul wrote, "And we know that for those who love God all things work together for good" (Romans 8:28 ESV).

Religion may not be the answer for everyone. I don't know if "religion" is even the answer for me. What I know is that I found immense healing first in finding out that Diane had wanted me, and then by trusting the stirrings of my reticent heart and giving it fully to my imperfect-but-endlessly-trying mom. Even if it had turned out that neither of my mothers had wanted me, realizing that God had been caring for me all along and was there to offer me the unconditional love I'd always longed for was the ultimate and extraordinary resolution to forty years of mother-longing. My sense of worthiness has radically changed. Even on my lowest days, I know definitively that I am adored. When I'm overcome with fear, I focus on God's light beaming inside of me. When I'm taking myself too seriously, I recall the gentle, loving chuckle of God and remember to laugh and play and create. When I struggle to belong or to be liked, I remember I'm a precious child of God. When I'm unsure, I stop my tendency toward busying around to listen for God ... and hope that I'm paying close enough attention to hear what he has to say.

I'm still baffled that God and I conversed the way we did while Mom was dying. I know it's not that way for everyone, and it hasn't been that way for me since. Maybe too many years had passed and too many generations had left too many important things unspoken. It was time to knock some spoken word into my head. Perhaps I needed to land at my most vulnerable, weary point in life to finally recognize the voice of God. As Shannan Martin writes, "But if we're willing to wake up to the world pulsing around us, if we're paying attention, we might be surprised."[3] But I wholeheartedly believe that God mothers us all, ready to wrap us up in divine mother-love if and when we're ready, however we're most apt to understand. Like Mom felt *a rescue is a rescue and a gift from above*, I have come to see that nurturing is nurturing and a gift from above.

As a writer and storyteller, my preferred means of communicating has always been through words. So I guess it makes sense that that's how God spoke to me — through the gift of words. Words that came together to tell a story. A story that helped me understand. A story that I feel so lucky to get to share. Thank you for letting me share it with you.

Butterfly Heaven

By Linda Easterly, presented to a
Mothers of Preschoolers (MOPS) group

Gosh. With everyone looking at me, I feel that I should begin with something astonishing. How about … I was born as a poor little urchin in a cabin in the Appalachian Mountains. Guess not. Actually, I was really born into a nice little Lutheran Swedish family in Minnesota.

I was raised to be a church attender. I think it was expected that automatically made me a Christian. But, like someone once said, "Being in a church doesn't make you a Christian any more than being in a garage makes you a car."

The fact is, I never paid much attention to what was being taught. I went because my parents made me. I did love "The Old Rugged Cross" and "Beautiful Savior" and to hear those other gorgeous old hymns from my dad's booming voice.

Like a lot of young people I quit going to church in college and didn't miss it much. We were Christmas and Easter pew sitters for quite a while.

Then along came Sara, our first daughter and an animal lover like you've never seen before. She even had Walter, a pet worm. He came to an unfortunate demise when she band-aided him to the deck so he'd wait for her to eat lunch. But it was 100 degrees. Oops. Lots of tears.

Well, one day Sara found a butterfly in the garage so she adopted her and named her Shirley. Unfortunately, despite all our efforts, the butterfly flew away at the first opportunity. So Sara became hysterical. I'd about had enough of the pet drama so I told her there was a butterfly heaven. She had no idea what I was talking about ... heaven? So I decided I'd send her to a Bible School at a nearby church ... the denomination was Dutch Reformed, which I'd never heard of. But, heck, they probably knew about butterfly heaven.

Well, Sara came home singing songs like, "I'm excited, I'm excited, I'm excited in the Lord. When you're walking with the Lord, ya don't get bored. Sing alleluia. Amen." Now, that was downright born-again stuff so I marched over there, I think to tell them a thing or two about butterfly heaven, or possibly religion. I pretty much knew everything when I was in my twenties.

But, there was a very wise pastor there, who loved a challenge and saw me coming. He talked me into joining the MOPS groups, one of the very first in the country. MOPS began right there in Littleton, Colorado. I attended because they were discussing Dr. Dobson's book, *Dare to Discipline*. Somehow at the classes I came to know God as a loving Savior who actually wanted a relationship with me. Soon I was attending church, reading a Bible, and felt change within.

Telling Bob about this was scary because I was always into the latest trend ... yoga, microwave cooking (back when they were about half the size of a refrigerator) or "stretch and sew" classes. And remember Jazzercize? So I made an appointment to talk to him so I wouldn't chicken out. I told him I decided to make Jesus Christ my Lord and Savior, fully expecting him to roll his eyes. All he said was, "I wondered what was different about you," and he started going to church with us.

Then a lot of years happened of just regular working life. I was a school teacher; Bob, a banker. We raised our kids and led a normal life, just proud as could be of our two kids as they graduated college and got married to a couple great guys.

Something else special happened in those years. Eight of my friends and I started Bible Study, which has lasted about thirty-three years. We have supported each other through divorces, teen pregnancies, a big legal mess, and a daughter's suicide. I came to cherish these friendships tremendously. We prayed each other through crisis after crisis.

UNTIL. I wonder if everyone has an UNTIL. Our first-born grandchild became very sick when she was a few months old. I still can't tell this whole story (the tears just start rolling), but our baby, Kenna, died at nine months old. I learned that a broken heart really does hurt. Our daughter, Amy (Kenna's mom), wrote a CaringBridge page every day, giving updates on her baby and writing out a Bible verse. She explained how that particular passage affected the day's events. Those caring pages provided some encouragement, yet it was hard to find comfort. I remember spending long, dark nights beside Kenna's crib just begging God to take me instead. After all, I had gotten a nice full life and my health was already compromised. Kenna hadn't gotten to really live yet. It was so difficult to trust God. Amy has been able to see God's plans and is grateful that she got to be Kenna's mom, even for a short time. I'm not there yet.

Slowly, very slowly, we started to live again. But I had been diagnosed with polymyositis, an autoimmune disease that attacks muscle. Through the five months of Kenna's hospitalization I had not taken care of myself ... mostly because I didn't care about myself. Amy and I often had a bag of gummy worms for lunch. That is when the polymyositis starting attacking my lungs.

Another UNTIL. Until it went into pulmonary fibrosis. It got hard to function ... and eventually I could not get from the kitchen to the bedroom. There is no known reason for the disease and no cure except lung transplant.

We started exploring the possibility of transplant, and ran into obstacle upon obstacle. After meeting with the first and second doctors in Pittsburgh and Gainesville, I said, "No way in the world that I'm having that surgery!" But fairly soon it became apparent that I no longer had a choice.

So we began the grueling process of day after day testing to see if I could be a candidate. I was judged to be an excellent candidate UNTIL it was discovered that to match lungs would be highly unlikely. First, I have Type B blood, which only nine percent of the population has. Far worse is that my disease had shrunk the lungs, which then shrunk the whole cavity. That meant I would need what the doctors call "midget lungs," probably from a child. On top of that I had 28 percent antibodies that had to be matched. I was pretty sure that lungs, hard as they are to obtain, would not be found for me.

Yup. I am the person that Pastor Dane began telling you about and requesting prayers. You were praying that I would receive a new pair of lungs before it was too late. I came here today just to thank you for those prayers, but then my whole story just came tumbling out of me.

As you know, the lungs came. Nearly a year ago.

When I went into that operating room, I swear I could SEE the prayers. It was a big room and the air was lavender and blue. I asked a nurse to just look. But she ignored me. I had not been drugged yet, and I remember all that was going on. Because the surgery can be so long, there're two shifts of workers talking and discussing their schedules. I kept trying to get their attention. I asked why they didn't tell me that blue was the attire color. Everyone had on blue except me. I had this silly-looking gown on with little pink bunnies. I even asked them why they were ignoring me. After all, this was MY party. I thought I was being hysterical, but they just put me to sleep.

I had no fear. None. I knew that this night could be the last night of my life or the first night of a whole new life. Either way was okay. I had my family waiting for me here; I had my dad and Kenna waiting for me in heaven.

My recovery was nothing short of miraculous. I had been told I'd be in Tampa for months. I went home in 11 days! I went to a Christmas party on my one-month anniversary. Since there have been some significant scares of rejection, and because I am so compromised, there have been some nasty infections. But so far I've conquered all the threats.

You know those women in my Bible Study I was telling you about? Well, in a couple weeks when we are back in Denver, they'll be giving me a one-year birthday party to celebrate my first year of new life. Even a cake! All nine of us will be together. But no oxygen tank.

Remember how Sara needed butterfly heaven? Last year at Christmas Bob gave me a pendant that would hide my trachea hole ... a butterfly! I assumed it represented my freedom. He thought it looked like lungs. Now I think it's to remind us of butterfly heaven. Just to reassure you, Sara did get a golden retriever a short while later who was her best friend for 13 years. So she didn't have to get pet worms anymore. And Amy had another baby — an active, precious little boy. And as for that church that didn't teach me anything? I went back to Hardin, Montana to visit it just a few years ago. And tears just streamed uncontrollably down my cheeks. I realized how many seeds were planted during all those Sundays. Far from being wasted, that time was preparing my heart to move into a meaningful level.

Does my story have a moral? Possibly what Pastor Dane tells us about adversity making us resilient and resilience giving us hope.

Possibly about encouraging everyone to consider becoming an organ donor. Possibly to affirm that praying for one another really is important, or possibly to encourage everyone to write their own story to see the way God orchestrated so many details.

But I've come to discover that God will allow these extreme lows in our lives to teach us that all we really need is Him. He is enough.

Acknowledgments

Thanks, most especially, to God, for caring so deeply about me—more than I will ever realize or could possibly deserve. Thank you for rescuing me and hopefully using my story to offer more good for the world. "And God saw that it was good." (Not perfect.)

Thank you to Mom and Dad, for your devoted parenting, unwavering faith, and inspiring commitment—to family, each other, and always to me. Turning some of the most painful parts of my life into art in order to tell a specific story—this one—leaves out many of the wonderful, equally real stories that have been a significant part of our family life. Thank you for your grace, understanding, support, and blessing in allowing me to share this part of my spiritual story and hopefully honor family, love, and God in the process.

To Amy, there's nobody else I'd want joining me on this journey we've been on as sisters, daughters, and now mothers. Thanks for modeling faithfulness and for your endless support of me. I am beyond blessed that you are my sister and closest friend.

A special thanks to my grandma, Betty, who had age 101 read an early draft of this manuscript even though it was a hard read. I appreciate the ways you have been there for me throughout my life offering love, support, prayers, pickles, cinnamon rolls, and cherished childhood stories of mine scrawled onto recipe cards.

Thanks to Aunt Carol for your generous love and unwavering support of both Mom and me. And thanks to my cousin Jenny—for your listening ear, Jungian and feminist perspective, and decades of shared family memories.

I am also thankful for my mother-in-law Willa and her mother, Muriel — my Canadian mother role models, who have gifted me with their wisdom, love, and stellar parenting examples.

It is with much love that I thank and honor Diane and Shirley. Finding you made me exponentially rich in caring mothers and strong women in my life. To Darla: I'm touched by our shared delight in rainbows and look forward to knowing you in heaven.

Thanks to my besties Sara Ohlin and Mary Balmaceda. I'm sorry that you also know what it is like to lose a mother too soon, and thank you for the countless ways you've been there for me as a grieving daughter, and as a mother and writer.

To my editorial team of Steve Parolini (a.k.a. The Novel Doctor) and Melanie M. Austin: thank you for your care and wisdom, and for the ways you pushed me toward greater meaning and clarity.

Professionally I owe gratitude to Dianne Grob, Amy Barker D'Alessandro, and Teresa Williams for supporting me on my heart's journey. Thanks to my doula, Sharon Muza, who gifted me with the confidence that I could not only birth two enormous babies, but actually become a mother, too. And for sharing the life-giving mantra: "Good enough is good enough."

Thanks to friends, readers, and writers with whom I could trust early drafts and excerpts, and who gave me encouragement and feedback along the way: Stacy Tate, Cory Goldhaber, Krista Daniel, Joy Neufeld, Tamara Strijack, Ivy Asamoah Lopez, Tyler Nelson, Jody Coulston, Jennifer Deutsch, Sundee Frazier, and Nancy Miller.

I will always be indebted to the teachers and mentors who have influenced my writing and publishing journey: Mrs. Shirley, Greg Luft, R.A. Salvatore, Peggy King Anderson, Meg Lippert, Kathryn Galbraith, Brenda Z. Guiberson, Gloria Kempton, Kirby Larson,

Linda Sue Park, Darcy Pattison, Michelle DeRusha, and Anne Heffron.

Thanks, of course, to Dr. Gordon Neufeld, for articulating a comprehensive and heart-centered paradigm of human attachment and development. I could say much more, but my hope is that this book is a tribute to all it has meant to me.

Thank you to Pastor Richard Dahlstrom for leading Bethany Community Church, my spiritual home that has offered a place of comfort, theological understanding, and peace following my mom's death.

I also want to express gratitude for Rebeca and the women from the women's group. I wouldn't go back in time to join a conflict group again, but honor that you gave your hearts to me, accepted mine, and supported me during some difficult emotional crossings.

I will forever give my heart to my daughters, Violet and Olive, and forever work to win and keep your hearts. Thank you for coming into my life, for letting me love you, know you, honor you, and cherish you. I am proud, honored, and blessed to be your mama.

I am ever grateful for my husband Jeff. I'm not always easy to love, but you love me anyway. You embody what it means to be loyal, caring, sensitive, supportive, and perfectly imperfect. Thank you for being on the journey with me. I love you and celebrate you.

To young Sara: I see you and I know you. You are precious. I am sorry it took me so long to share your voice.

Notes

INTRODUCTION

1. Rachel Held Evans, *Inspired: Slaying Giants, Walking on Water, and Loving the Bible Again* (Nashville: Thomas Nelson, 2018), 44.

2. Nancy Newton Verrier, *Coming Home to Self: The Adopted Child Grows Up* (Baltimore: Gateway Press, Inc., 2003), 31.

3. Evans, *Inspired*, 221.

CHAPTER ONE: TAKING FLIGHT

1. Maggie Callanan and Patricia Kelley, *Final Gifts: Understanding the Special Awareness, Needs, and Communications of the Dying* (New York: Simon & Schuster Paperbacks, 1992), 74.

2. Ibid., 85.

3. Ibid., 97.

4. Betty Jean Lifton, *Lost & Found: The Adoption Experience*, 3rd. ed. (Ann Arbor: The University of Michigan Press, 2009), 54.

CHAPTER TWO: BUTTERFLY DELIVERANCE

1. Verrier, *Coming Home to Self*, 354.

2. Gordon Neufeld, Ph.D., "Session Five: The Counterwill Storm," *Making Sense of Adolescence* (class lecture, Neufeld Institute, Vancouver, BC, 2011), DVD.

CHAPTER THREE: UNWANTED

1. Lifton, *Lost & Found*, 21.

2. Ibid., 22–23.

CHAPTER FOUR: STORM RUNNER

1. Verrier, *Coming Home to Self*, 58.

CHAPTER FIVE: IDEATIONS

1. Margaret A. Keyes, Stephen M. Malone, Anu Sharma, William G. Iacono and Matt McGue, "Risk of Suicide Attempt in Adopted and Nonadopted Offspring," *Pediatrics*, (September 9, 2013), 2012-3251, http://pediatrics.aappublications.org/content/early/2013/09/04/peds.2012-3251.

CHAPTER SEVEN: CHRYSALIS CRISIS

1. Gordon Neufeld, Ph.D., "Session One: Becoming Attached," *The Art & Science of Transplanting Children,* (class lecture, Neufeld Institute, Vancouver, BC, 2011), DVD.

2. Neufeld, "Session Five: Impediments to Re-Attachment: Protective Shyness," *The Art & Science of Transplanting Children.*

CHAPTER EIGHT: LOVE LONGING

1. C.S. Lewis, *The Four Loves,* reissue ed. (San Francisco: HarperOne, 2017), 155.

CHAPTER SEVENTEEN: CAMOUFLAGE REMOVAL

1. Brené Brown, Ph.D., "Listening to Shame" filmed March 2012, TED video, 20:24, https://www.ted.com/talks/brene_brown_listening_to_shame.

CHAPTER TWENTY-FIVE: MOTHER WHINERS

1. Nancy Newton Verrier, *The Primal Wound: Understanding the Adopted Child* (Baltimore: Gateway Press, Inc., 1993), 154.

2. Verrier, *Coming Home to Self,* 74.

CHAPTER TWENTY-SIX: DRAMA DESIRE

1. Verrier, *The Primal Wound,* 96.

2. Verrier, *Coming Home to Self,* 71.

3. Alexandra Stein, *Terror, Love, and Brainwashing: Attachment in Cults and Totalitarian Systems* (New York: Routledge, 2017), 133.

CHAPTER TWENTY-SEVEN: TRANSPLANTING TROUBLE

1. Neufeld, "Session Five," *The Art and Science of Transplanting Children.*

2. Verrier, *The Primal Wound,* 14.

3. Neufeld, "Session Five," *The Art and Science of Transplanting Children.*

4. Robert Karen, Ph.D., *Becoming Attached: First Relationships and How They Shape Our Capacity to Love* (New York: Oxford University Press, 1998), 100.

5. Verrier, *The Primal Wound,* 96.

CHAPTER TWENTY-EIGHT: PRODIGAL DAUGHTER

1. Gordon Neufeld, Ph.D., "Working with Stuck Kids," *Neufeld Intensive I: Making Sense of Kids* (home study guide, Neufeld Institute, Vancouver, BC, 2007), 28.

2. Verrier, *Coming Home to Self,* 338.

3. Ibid., 339.

CHAPTER TWENTY-NINE: THE VULNERABLE PATH TO FORGIVENESS

1. Blythe Daniel and Helen McIntosh, *Mended: Restoring the Hearts of Mothers and Daughters* (Eugene: Harvest House Publishers, 2019), 17.

2. Callanan and Kelley, *Final Gifts*, 155–165.

CHAPTER THIRTY-ONE: MAKING IT

1. Verrier, *Coming Home to Self*, 17.

2. Ibid., 317.

3. Ibid., 324.

CHAPTER THIRTY-THREE: ONLY ME

1. Verrier, *Coming Home to Self*, 312.

CHAPTER THIRTY-FOUR: A NEW LIFELINE

1. Richard Dahlstrom, *Encounters with Christ 3*: "Learning from Storms," sermon at Bethany Community Church, July 29, 2018, Seattle Washington.

2. Verrier, *The Primal Wound*, 11–12.

CHAPTER THIRTY-FIVE: ALPHA & OMEGA

1. Gordon Neufeld, Ph.D., "Session One: Making Sense of Alpha," *Alpha Children: Reclaiming Our Rightful Place in Their Lives* (class lecture, Neufeld Institute, Vancouver, BC, 2013), DVD.

2. Neufeld, "Session Three: The Causes and Consequences of an Alpha Complex," *Alpha Children*.

3. Thomas Lewis, M.D., Fari Amini, M.D., Richard Lannon, M.D., *A General Theory of Love* (New York: Vintage Books/Random House, Inc., 2000), 97.

4. Neufeld, "Session Three," *Alpha Children*.

5. Verrier, *Coming Home to Self*, 467.

CHAPTER THIRTY-SIX: I FELT THE LIGHT

1. Diana L. Hayes, *No Crystal Stair: Womanist Spirituality* (Maryknoll, NY: Orbis Books, 2016), 35–36. Excerpt accessible in Richard Rohr's "The River Flows" published August 2, 2019 https://cac.org/the-river-flows-2019-08-02/

2. Deanna Shrodes, "Affected by Adoption—Body, Soul, and Spirit." Published on the *Lost Daughters* blog, January 19, 2013. Accessible at http://www.thelostdaughters.com/2013/01/affected-by-adoption-body-soul-spirit.html

CHAPTER THIRTY-EIGHT: LOOKING UP

1. Verrier, *Coming Home to Self*, 50.

2. Hayes, *No Crystal Stair*, 35–36.

3. Kelley Nikondeha, *Adopted: The Sacrament of Belonging in a Fractured World* (Grand Rapids: William B. Eerdmans Publishing Company, 2017), 20.

CHAPTER THIRTY-NINE: WRITING MR. RIGHT

1. Stanley Hauerwas, "Sex and Politics: Bertrand Russell and 'Human Sexuality.'" Accessible at http://www.religion-online.org/article/sex-andpolitics-bertrand-russell-and-human-sexuality/

CHAPTER FORTY: SAVING THE WORLD

1. Neufeld, "Session Two: The Many Faces of Alpha," *Alpha Children*.

CHAPTER FORTY-ONE: FOOTPRINTS

1. Nikondeha, *Adopted*, 36.

EPILOGUE

1. Evans, *Inspired*, 217.

2. Jo Jones, Ph.D. and Paul Placek, Ph.D., *Adoption: By the Numbers: A Comprehensive Report on U.S. Adoption Statistics* (National Council For Adoption, 2017). Accessible at https://www.adoptioncouncil.org/publications/2017/02/adoption-by-the-numbers

3. Shannan Martin, *The Ministry of Ordinary Places* (Nashville: Nelson Books, 2018), 24.